Robert Bresson

MANCHESTER
UNIVERSITY PRESS

FRENCH FILM DIRECTORS

DIANA HOLMES and ROBERT INGRAM *series editors*
DUDLEY ANDREW *series consultant*

Luc Besson SUSAN HAYWARD

Claude Chabrol GUY AUSTIN

Diane Kurys CARRIE TARR

George Méliès ELIZABETH EZRA

Coline Serreau BRIGITTE ROLLET

François Truffaut DIANA HOLMES AND ROBERT INGRAM

Agnès Varda ALISON SMITH

forthcoming titles

Jean-Jacques Beineix PHIL POWRIE

Bertrand Blier SUE HARRIS

Jean Cocteau JAMES WILLIAMS

Marguerite Duras RENATE GUNTHER

Jean-Luc Godard STEVE CANNON AND ELIANE MEYER

Jean Renoir MARTIN O'SHAUGHNESSY

Bertrand Tavernier LYNN A. HIGGINS

André Teclimé BILL MARSHALL

Jean Vigo MICHAEL TEMPLE

FRENCH FILM DIRECTORS

Robert Bresson

KEITH READER

Manchester University Press

MANCHESTER AND NEW YORK

distributed exclusively in the USA by St. Martin's Press

Published by Manchester University Press
Oxford Road, Manchester M13 9NR, UK
and Room 400, 175 Fifth Avenue, New York, NY 10010, USA
http://www.man.ac.uk/mup

Distributed exclusively in the USA by
St. Martin's Press, Inc., 175 Fifth Avenue, New York,
NY 10010, USA

Distributed exclusively in Canada by
UBC Press, University of British Columbia, 2029 West Mall,
Vancouver, BC, Canada v6T 1z2

British Library Cataloguing-in-Publication Data
A catalogue record for this book is available from the British Library

Library of Congress Cataloging-in-Publication Data applied for

ISBN 0 7190 5365 x *hardback*
     0 7190 5366 8 *paperback*

First published 2000

07 06 05 04 03 02 01 00   10 9 8 7 6 5 4 3 2 1

Typeset in Scala with Meta display
by Koinonia, Manchester
Printed in Great Britain
by Biddles Ltd, Guildford and King's Lynn

Contents

List of plates

Plates 1–8 courtesy of the Collection Robert et Mylène Bresson. Plate 9 courtesy of SYGMA.

Series editors' foreword

To an anglophone audience, the combination of the words 'French' and 'cinema' evokes a particular kind of film: elegant and wordy, sexy but serious – an image as dependent on national stereotypes as is that of the crudely commercial Hollywood blockbuster, which is not to say that either image is without foundation. Over the past two decades, this generalised sense of a significant relationship between French identity and film has been explored in scholarly books and articles, and has entered the curriculum at university level and, in Britain, at A-level. The study of film as an art-form and (to a lesser extent) as industry, has become a popular and widespread element of French Studies, and French cinema has acquired an important place within Film Studies. Meanwhile, the growth in multi-screen and 'art-house' cinemas, together with the development of the video industry, has led to the greater availability of foreign-language films to an English-speaking audience. Responding to these developments, this series is designed for students and teachers seeking information and accessible but rigorous critical study of French cinema, and for the enthusiastic filmgoer who wants to know more.

The adoption of a director-based approach raises questions about *auteurism*. A series that categorises films not according to period or to genre (for example), but to the person who directed them, runs the risk of espousing a romantic view of film as the product of solitary inspiration. On this model, the critic's role might seem to be that of discovering continuities, revealing a necessary coherent set of themes and motifs which correspond to the particular genius of the individual. This is not our aim: the *auteur* perspective on film, itself most clearly articulated in France in the early 1950s, will be interrogated in certain volumes of the series, and, throughout, the director will be treated as one highly significant element in a complex process of film production and reception which includes socio-economic and political determinants, the work of a large and highly skilled team of artists and technicians, the mechanisms of production and distribution, and the complex and multiply determined responses of spectators.

The work of some of the directors in the series is already known outside France, that of others is less so – the aim is both to provide informative and original English-language studies of established figures, and to extend the range of French directors known to anglophone students of cinema. We intend the series to contribute to the promotion of the informal and formal study of French films, and to the pleasure of those who watch them.

DIANA HOLMES

ROBERT INGRAM

Preface

I began teaching French cinema in a British university – then called a polytechnic – in 1975, during the pre-video era when 16-millimetre prints were screened to groups of students. The course, shared with a colleague, adopted, like this series, an *auteur*-based approach, and Bresson was one of six directors studied. I knew his work very little at the outset and did not care much for most of what I did know, so that the bulk of the teaching of his films fell to my colleague, fortunately an ardent enthusiast. *Mouchette* (1967), and even to an extent *Journal d'un curé de campagne* (1951), intrigued me by their tight visual organisation and depiction of the miseries of life in the depths of provincial France, but as that most oxymoronic of entities an ex-Catholic, I was unsurprisingly as resistant to the redemptive ending of *Pickpocket* (1959) as to the odyssey of meekness in *Au hasard Balthazar* (1966), which struck me as little more than *Black Beauty* with a strong dose of opium of the people thrown in.

That all changed in the spring of 1982, when study-leave arrangements meant that I taught the whole of the French cinema course, including Bresson. The family and personal circumstances that catalysed my change are less important than the dramatic manner of its occurrence. As the cross filled the silent screen at the end of *Journal d'un curé de campagne* (hereinafter *Journal*), I left the room in tears, and even more extraordinarily the same thing occurred – the same tears happened to me – at the end of *Pickpocket*, a film whose laconic style I had hitherto dismissed as meretricious.

Paul Schrader has identified a key Bressonian moment as that of the 'decisive action', which 'forces the viewer into the confrontation with the Wholly Other he would normally avoid' (Schrader 1972: 81). That confrontation enacts on the other side of the screen the decisive action carried out – often in spite of themselves – by the films' central characters, so that my experience on re-viewing Bresson's films had all but made of me one of their protagonists, bringing about a performative identification that had less to do with *who* those protagonists were (I had stolen only infrequently and never been a priest) than with *where*. Within a week of the screenings that had so moved me, I had drafted an outline for a research proposal and submitted it to the British Academy for funding. I spent a month of that summer in the film libraries of Paris, saturating myself in Bressoniana, and the resulting article (Reader, 1986) became the first one on film to be published by the journal *French Studies*.

I mention this not (only) out of boastfulness or in order to substantiate my bona fides as a Bresson scholar, but because the extraordinary speed with which I moved from scepticism, verging on hostility, to passionate professional and personal commitment remains unprecedented in my experience. Extraordinary too was the coincidence that in his major book on Bresson, published in the same year as my article, Philippe Arnaud deploys the selfsame quotation from the Judaeo-Christian mystic Simone Weil that I had used – 'La grâce comble, mais elle ne peut entrer que là où il y a un vide pour la recevoir, et c'est elle qui fait ce vide'[1] (Weil 1988: 18; Arnaud 1986: 20; Reader 1986: 441). Less extraordinary than it may at first seem, perhaps – Weil's sparse, aphoristic writing is easily read as a pre-text for Bresson's own *Notes sur le cinématographe*, and the importance of grace in the Bressonian universe is recognised by virtually all commentators on him – but an indication nonetheless of how my view of that universe interacted with others'. My fascination with Bresson's work is largely a fascination with the variety of critical discourses, ranging from the adulatory to the scornful, it has generated, and in the pages that follow I shall try to give due space to these as well as to the films themselves.

My thanks go to: the New Professors' Fund of the University of Newcastle upon Tyne for funding a period of sustained research in Paris; the Maison Suger in Paris for providing accommodation during that period; the staff of the Bibliothèque du Film, the Bibliothèque de l'Arsenal and the Bibliothèque François Mitterrand in Paris, and of the British Film Institute Library in London, for their kind and informed help; the Cinémathèque de Paris for making it possible for me to view three Bresson films (*Affaires publiques* (1934), *Une femme douce* (1969) and *Quatre nuits d'un rêveur* (1972)) otherwise unavailable; the Institut National de l'Audiovisuel (INA) for arranging a screening of the television programme on Bresson *Pour le plaisir*; Liz Andersen, Mylène Bresson, Rachel Edwards, Jill Forbes, Jean-Pierre Jeancolas, Chris Johnson, Eleonore Kofman, Catherine O'Brien, Phil Powrie, Ken Richardson, Naomi Segal, Trista Selous, Ginette Vincendeau and Anne Wiazemsky for their help, support and advice.

References

Arnaud, Philippe (1986), *Robert Bresson*, Paris, Cahiers du Cinéma.

Reader, Keith (1998), '"D'où cela vient-il?": notes on three films by Robert Bresson', in James Quandt (ed.), *Robert Bresson*, Cinematheque Ontario, Toronto.

Schrader, Paul (1972), *Transcendental Style in Film: Ozu, Bresson, Dreyer*, Los Angeles/London, University of California Press.

Weil, Simone (1988), *La Pesanteur et la grâce*, Paris, Plon.

[1] 'Grace fills up, but it can enter only where there is an empty space to receive it, and it makes this empty space itself.'

Introduction

'Bresson est "à part" dans ce métier terrible',[1] according to Jean Cocteau (Cocteau 1997: 35). Cocteau's chosen epithet runs like a leitmotif through fifty years' and more evaluation and description of Bresson's work. Whether hagiographic, contemptuous or somewhere in between, those writers and critics, from Marguerite Duras to Patti Smith, who have dealt with Bresson have been almost unanimous in their assertion of his uniqueness – sometimes, it might be thought, acting as a pretext for avoiding or curtailing further analysis of his work. Immense though his influence on other directors has been – Jean Eustache, Rainer Werner Fassbinder, Philippe Garrel, Jean-Luc Godard, Aki Kaurismäki among Europeans; in transatlantic cinema, Atom Egoyan, Hal Hartley, Monte Hellman, Martin Scorsese[2] – Bresson himself passes for the archetypally uninfluenced film-maker, a myth reinforced by his insistence that he never goes to the cinema ('Hier encore, quelqu'un me disait (c'est un reproche qu'on me fait parfois, sans le vouloir, mais c'en est un): "Pourquoi n'allez-vous jamais voir les films?" Car c'est absolument vrai: je ne vais pas les voir.' (Ndlr: Bresson va voir tous les films)[3] (Godard and Delahaye 1966: 32, 71).

1 'Bresson is "apart" in this terrible trade.'
2 A useful overview of Bresson's influence on three major film-makers – Jean Eustache, Philippe Garrel and Monte Hellman – is to be found in Brenez (1996a). Quandt (1998) includes seventy variously provocative and hagiographic observations by 'Filmmakers on Bresson' (523–91).
3 'Only yesterday somebody was saying to me (it's an unintentional criticism

This individualism articulates itself through an instantly recognisable visual style – pared-down, laconic, elliptical – and a non- (or sometimes hyper-) realist use of sound and voice. 'Lorsqu'un son peut remplacer une image, supprimer l'image ou la neutraliser'⁴ (Bresson [1975] 1988: 62). Jonathan Rosenbaum, indeed, has identified 'sound presence', along with 'the framed image', as the two major reasons why he believes that Bresson's work does not successfully translate to video (Rosenbaum 1998: 17). The intense focus on key sounds, such as the raking of the leaves in the scene between the priest and the countess in *Journal* or the racecourse ticket-machines in *Pickpocket*, is complemented by a vocal delivery which often makes it sound as if the characters were quoting their lines rather than speaking them. Even the term 'characters', in that sentence, is open to doubt; a *Cinéma 63* symposium on Bresson yielded the following exchange:

> (Michel Mesnil) ... Il n'y a pas un seul personnage féminin sympathique chez Bresson.
> (Robert Benayoun) Il n'y a pas de personnages sympathiques chez Bresson.
> (Pierre Billard) Y a-t-il des personnages chez Bresson?
>
> (*Cinéma 63*: 27)⁵

The absence – increasingly marked in the later works – of the kind of psychological detail and motivation that characterises a no less spiritually intense film-maker such as Bergman makes it genuinely tempting to proffer 'No' as an answer to that final question. Bresson's characters tend to come without the baggage of information, direct or indirect, we might expect from other directors; we know nothing of the priest's parents in *Journal* or of Michel's previous life or occupation in *Pickpocket*, the couple in *Une femme douce* are never given names, the provincial region in which the action of *Au hasard Balthazar* (hereinafter *Balthazar*) is

sometimes made of me, but a criticism all the same): "Why don't you ever go to see films?" That's absolutely correct – I never go to see them' (Editorial footnote: Bresson always goes to see films).
4 'When a sound can replace an image, get rid of the image or neutralise it.'
5 'There is not a single sympathetic female character in Bresson. There are no sympathetic characters in Bresson. Are there any characters in Bresson?'

set is never specified in the film (other than obliquely through a car number-plate). This absence of detail – hence, of 'character' in the sense in which a Balzac or a Renoir would have understood it – is commented upon by virtually every writer on Bresson, whether hostile as when John Coleman describes *Balthazar* as 'almost comical in its withholding of information' (Coleman 1969: 86) or more soberly analytical as in P. Adams Sitney's view that Bresson 'thoroughly empties out the projection of intention, conflict, and other signs of interiority'. For Sitney, he 'invests the act of seeing – and therefore the shot-countershot structure – with the full burden of fictional psychology' (Sitney 1998b: 150). This displacement of 'content' onto 'form' helps to explain the interest in Bresson's work shown by such formally conscious writers on and in film as Jean-Pierre Oudart, Jean-Marie Straub and Danièle Huillet or Susan Sontag. That interest does not so much elide or marginalise the specifically Catholic aspects of the films as subsume them within the formal dimension. For Peter Schofer, 'two avatars, rhetoric and Jansenism, are condensed in the films of Bresson' (Schofer 1974: 59), and it is that condensation that provides the key to understanding how writers out of sympathy with a Catholic perspective, such as those mentioned above, have approached his work. According to René Prédal, the commonest Bressonian rhetorical figures are litotes, ellipsis and metonymy (Prédal 1992: 30), the first of these associated above all with sexual love (Bresson's work is saturated with sexual tension yet contains nothing that resembles a 'sex scene', with the possible exception of *Quatre nuits d'un rêveur*). Ellipsis, in the form of unanswered questions (*Pickpocket*) or gaps in the narrative (*Balthazar*), works against conventional psychology and its overtones of filmed theatre, while metonymy – the shawl in the opening sequence of *Une femme douce*, the armour in *Lancelot du lac* (1974) – appears more marked in the colour films, whose tendency towards greater expansiveness it works to contain.

Bresson's refusal, from *Journal* onwards, of professional actors (Anne Wiazemsky and Dominique Sanda went on to successful acting careers, but never appeared for Bresson again) is of a piece with his rejection of psychology and character. He goes so far as to refuse the very word 'acteur', preferring to speak of 'modèles', a term whose overtones of automatism and malleability are significant:

> Modèle. Questionné (par les gestes que tu lui fais faire, les mots que tu lui fais dire). Réponse (quand ce ne serait qu'un refus de répondre) que souvent tu ne perçois pas mais que la caméra enregistre. Soumise *ensuite* à ton étude.[6]

The notorious frequency with which Bresson obliges his *modèles*[7] to repeat their lines and gestures (up to fifty times), and his insistence that they eschew any apparent emotional investment in or colouring of what they say, become understandable in this context. Only afterwards, on screen during editing, away from the gaze of the *modèles* who have no access to the process, does it become plain which version is the 'right' one, the one that has achieved in its relationship with other words and images what Roland Barthes calls the *punctum* to which ultimately the whole film will owe its force. It is in this sense that we should understand René Briot's view that 'pour Bresson, [l'image] n'a qu'une valeur d'échange'[8] (Briot 1957: 23).

Bresson's use of *modèles*, so far as I know unique in the cinema, suggests three approaches to his work to which I shall return in this study. It smacks, first, of a sadism unappealingly distilled in his remark to Paul Guth during the shooting of *Les Dames du bois de Boulogne* (1945) (hereinafter *Les Dames*) that '[i]l faut apprivoiser son sujet comme un homme apprivoise sa femme'[9] (Guth 1989: 106); his frequent squabbles with Maria Casarès during *Les Dames*, Claude Laydu's pulling a medallion from a real fire in the shooting of *Journal*, Marie Cardinal's description of the filming of *Mouchette* (Cardinal 1967) all provide anecdotal evidence for this,

---

6 'Model. Questioned (by the gestures you make him carry out, the words you make him say). A response (even if only a refusal to respond) that you often do not perceive but that is recorded by your camera. Only then is it submitted to your scrutiny.'

7 I use the French term throughout to emphasise the particularity of Bresson's terminology.

8 'For Bresson, [the image] has only exchange value.'

9 'You have to tame your subject-matter as a man tames his woman.'

though Anne Wiazemsky is insistent that he was a delight to work for. Jean-Pierre Oudart goes so far as to theorise the 'rapport sadien entre le séducteur et sa victime' as the 'inscription refoulée des rapports établis au cours du tournage du film entre le metteur en scène et ses acteurs (ses actrices)'[10] (Oudart 1972: 88). Sternberg and Hitchcock are precedents that may occur to us here, but the iconographising thrust of the one and the bullying, overgrown-schoolboy playfulness of the other are a long way from what Bresson seeks to achieve. Almost like the surrealists with their interest in automatic writing, he uses repetition and reiteration to strip away layers of self-defence masquerading as self-projection – the quality he so abhors in conventional screen acting – and accede to an unconscious truth in which his *modèles'* 'rapports avec les personnes et les objets autour d'eux seront *justes*, parce qu'ils ne seront pas *pensés*'[11] (Bresson [1976] 1988: 34–5). We are here close to the second of the approaches I have mentioned – a view of the unconscious associated with Freud and more particularly with Lacan, that Lacan who 'denigrates "humanistic" philosophy and psychology that treat man as an actor who wills his action and instead sees man as a submitting object of processes that transcend him' (Turkle 1979: 49–50). Bresson's relation to his *modèles* appears in many respects like that of the analyst to his or her analysands ('l'important n'est pas ce qu'ils me montrent mais ce qu'ils cachent, et surtout *ce qu'ils ne savent pas qui est en eux*'[12] – Bresson [1976] 1988: 17), and recent Bresson scholarship (the work of Philippe Arnaud and Jean-Pierre Oudart in particular) has drawn largely on Lacanian concepts and methods.

Lacanian discourse has a complex and multiply determined relationship with Catholicism, and – third and last, but emphatically not least, in my short list of common approaches – Bresson has the reputation of being the cinema's greatest Catholic director

10 'The Sadean relationship between the seducer and his victim [is] the repressed inscription of the relationships set up during shooting between the director and his actors and actresses.'

11 '[Their] relationships with the people and objects around them will be *true*, because they will not be *thought through*.'

12 'The important thing is not what they show me, but what they hide from me, and above all *what they do not know is in them*.'

(doubtless leaving Dreyer and Bergman to fight it out for the Protestant crown). For Louis Malle writing on *Pickpocket*, '[p]endant le temps de la projection, l'artiste est Dieu'[13] (*Éloge* 1997: 36) – we may think, bearing in mind the celebrated Lacanian *boutade* 'je père-sévère',[14] God the Father (*primus inter pares* if ever there were) at that. Catholic artists – François Mauriac and, even more, Graham Greene are the best-known examples – have a wealth of experience in recasting sinners as saints, so that the exceptionally high incidence of suicides in Bresson (four in thirteen features)[15] situates him within a well-established heretical tradition. The theological term most often used to refer to Bresson, however, is Jansenist, after the Dutch theologian whose belief in predestination set him at odds with orthodox Catholicism. Jansenism, influential in France through the work of Racine and Pascal, has as its founding premise the radical hiddenness of God, at once present within yet absent from the world we perceive and thus able to be recognised only by those destined from all eternity to do so. Susan Sontag (Sontag 1969) was probably the first critic to suggest the analogies between the often violently heterodox Christian thought of Pascal and Simone Weil on the one hand and Bresson's on the other. Weil's observation on the void created by the action of grace[16] quite literally mirrors Pascal, himself quoting God, when he writes '"tu ne me chercherais pas, si tu ne m'avais trouvé"'[17] (Pascal [1670] 1976: 200).

Pascal's wager on the existence of God has what contemporary linguistics might call a performative effect, for it is only thanks to the wager that God's existence becomes certain and available to the believer. This means that the wager rests less on a craven calculation of self-interest than on the fact that God, if he exists, is

13 'For the time it takes to screen the film, the artist is God.'
14 Literally, 'I persevere,' but also 'I am a/the severe father.' A *boutade* is a witty remark.
15 To wit: Doctor Delbende in *Journal*, Mouchette and the *femme douce* in the films of those names, and Charles in *Le Diable probablement*. (I have thus not counted marginal cases such as the country priest's self-neglect or Joan of Arc's recantation).
16 Quoted above, footnote 1, p. x.
17 '"You would not be seeking me if you had not already found me."'

qua infinite being necessarily hidden from and only partially, 'through a glass darkly', perceptible to the finite run of mortals.[18] God figures surprisingly little in Bresson's *œuvre*, and less and less as it unfolds, all but dispossessed by Satan by the time we reach *Le Diable probablement* (1977). His presence is most obtrusive as the tyrannical father-figure in whose name the death-dealing proceedings of *Le Procès de Jeanne d'Arc* (1962) (hereinafter *Procès*) take place; his absence – which turns out to have been a real presence all along – most laceratingly felt in *Journal* ('Dieu s'est retiré de moi, je suis sûr',[19] the priest says at one point); his presence-in-absence most movingly experienced perhaps in *Un condamné à mort s'est échappé* (1956) (hereinafter *Condamné*), described by Bresson himself in conversation as the film of grace *par excellence*, whose subtitle *Le Vent souffle où il veut* ('The wind bloweth where it listeth') distils the spirit of Jansenism.

If two of Bresson's first three feature films – *Les Anges du péché* and *Journal* – take the religious life as their setting, that life, like the God that is its ostensible inspiration, subsequently dwindles to near-invisibility. Few Catholic artists, however, have found the institutional life of 'their' Church a congenial or inspirational topic, and its declining importance in Bresson's later work is not of itself particularly surprising. That his work becomes more pessimistic in the course of his career is scarcely open to doubt, but the deepening disenchantment it shows with developments in contemporary society, from the *blousons noirs* in *Balthazar* to the environmental ravages depicted in *Le Diable probablement*, may not of itself be enough to justify its blanket labelling as 'pessimistic'.

My approach will be a chronological one – partly because in an *auteur*-based series that is the line of least resistance, but also because the patterns of evolution I have just described seem to me to lend themselves to it particularly well. I shall devote somewhat more space to *Balthazar* than to any of the other films, partly because I believe it to be Bresson's most important work and

18 Lucien Goldmann's *Le Dieu caché* (Goldmann, 1967) gives a masterly exposition of the importance for Pascal and Racine of God's essential hiddenness.
19 'God has gone away from me, I am sure.'

partly because of its unusual narrative complexity. Philippe Arnaud's description of his approach to 'la chaîne logique dont on peut suivre le fil à travers les films de Bresson' is one that I shall try to follow: 'chronologiquement, à travers les transformations, acteurs remplacés par des modèles, fragmentation, retard d'identification ... et esthétiquement par la constitution de son *"antisystème"*, de sa méthode'.[20] Finally, and as I have already suggested, my readings of the films will try to take their Catholic dimensions into account without rendering them inaccessible to those with no interest in, knowledge of or sympathy for Catholicism.

Biography

Comparatively little is known of Bresson's life, though such information as there is is largely uncontentious. The major discord, curiously, surrounds the year of his birth – 1901 or 1907 depending on the source. He was born in the province of Auvergne, went to secondary school in Sceaux (a well-off, residential suburb of Paris), where he specialised in Latin, Greek and philosophy, and initially planned a career as a painter, which he abandoned for reasons of nervous tension. Although painterly influences on his work, from Philippe de Champaigne to Cézanne, are frequently cited and he has often spoken of himself as primarily a painter, I have never seen, or even read a description of, a painting by him. His first film, the half-hour comedy *Affaires publiques*, was made in 1934, with money lent by the British associate of the surrealists, Roland Penrose. He was not to return to directing until *Les Anges du péché* in 1943, the first of only thirteen features he was to make over a period of forty years. Between 1933 and 1939 he collaborated on a number of films, none now readily available. He wrote dialogues for Fred Zelnik and Maurice Gleize's *C'était un musicien* (1933), worked on the adaptation of Saint-Exupéry's novel *Courrier*

---

20 'The logical chain which can be followed through Bresson's films: [...] chronologically, through his various transformations – actors replaced by models, fragmentation, delayed identification ... and aesthetically through the constitution of his "anti-system" or method'.

du sud filmed by Pierre Billon in 1936 and on the script of the intriguingly titled *Les Jumeaux de Brighton* for Claude Heymann (also 1936), was Henri Diamant-Berger's assistant on *La Vierge folle* (1938) and was helping with preparations for René Clair's *L'Air pur* when the film had to be abandoned because of the outbreak of war.[21]

He passed a year in captivity in Germany at the beginning of the war, which clearly served as an inspiration for *Condamné* but about which otherwise he does not appear to have spoken. His film-making career has been marked by difficulty in obtaining funding (often the result of his supposed intransigence); *Lancelot du lac*, released in 1974, had been a major project of his since just after *Journal*, and his lifelong dream of filming the Book of Genesis (*La Genèse*) has never been fulfilled. His quality of 'apartness' (to echo Cocteau) has meant that it is impossible to identify him unequivocally with any of the major tendencies of French film-making. An unusually high number of his films are adaptations of canonical literary texts – two (*Journal* and *Mouchette*) from Bernanos, two from Dostoevsky (*Une femme douce* and *Quatre nuits d'un rêveur*) and one apiece from Diderot (*Les Dames*) and Tolstoy (*L'Argent* (1983)) – yet his work is at the antipodes of the *cinéma de qualité* tradition that might appear to suggest. Beloved of *Cahiers du cinéma* and thus of the New Wave, his work was much more equivocally received by the amalgam of Marxists and surrealists associated with the other major French film journal *Positif*. Bernard Chardère published three highly appreciative pieces on him in the early days of *Positif*, but the vehement anti-clericalism of that journal was subsequently to lead to extremely cutting and hostile judgements by the likes of Robert Benayoun and Louis Seguin. It was not until 1996 and the publication of a 'Dossier Robert Bresson' in the December issue of the journal (74–103) that *Positif* can be said to have made its peace with Bresson, whose response to its earlier criticisms is not recorded.

21 I have culled this information from René Prédal's special number of *L'Avant-scène du cinéma* (Prédal 1992: 2).

In 1975 he published a short collection of aphoristic observations on the cinema, *Notes sur le cinématographe*, reissued in
1988 with a preface by the novelist Jean-Marie le Clézio. There
were plans for a second volume, but this has never come to pass.
He died in December 1999. He was twice married and once
widowed; his second wife was Mylène (née Van der Mersch),
assistant director on his work from *Quatre nuits d'un rêveur*
onwards. He had no children. For a great many years he divided
his time between a Parisian town house on the Ile Saint-Louis and
a country home near Chartres, though latterly poor health and
infirmity meant that he rarely left the countryside. Outside his
film-making, his life appears to have been uneventful. The films,
however, are all incontestably events in the history of French
cinema, as we shall now see.

References

Arnaud, Philippe (1986), *Robert Bresson*, Paris, Cahiers du Cinéma.
Brenez, Nicole (1996), '"Approche inhabituelle des corps"', *Positif*, no. 430.
Bresson, Robert ([1975] 1988), *Notes sur le cinématographe*, Paris, Gallimard.
Briot, René (1957), *Robert Bresson*, Paris, Cerf.
Cardinal, Marie (1967), *Cet été-là*, Paris, Julliard.
Cinéma 63, no. 73.
Cocteau, Jean (1997), in *Robert Bresson: Éloge* (1997), Milan/Paris, Mazzotta/Cinéma-
    thèque française.
Coleman, John (1969), '*Au hasard Balthazar*', in Ian Cameron (ed.), *The Films of
    Robert Bresson*, London, Studio Vista.
Godard, Jean-Luc, and Delahaye, Michel, (1966), 'La Question', *Cahiers du cinéma*,
    no. 178.
Goldmann, Lucien (1967), *Le Dieu caché*, Paris, Gallimard.
Guth, Paul (1989), *Autour des 'Dames du bois de Boulogne'*, Paris, Ramsay.
Malle, Louis (1997), '*Pickpocket*', in *Robert Bresson: Éloge*, Milan/Paris, Mazzotta/
    Cinémathèque française.
Oudart, Jean-Pierre (1972), 'Le Hors-champ de l'auteur', *Cahiers du cinéma*, nos. 236–7.
Pascal, Blaise ([1670] 1976), *Pensées*, Paris, GF-Flammarion.
Prédal, René (1992), *Robert Bresson: l'aventure intérieure*, *L'Avant-scène cinéma*, nos.
    408–9.
Quandt, James (ed.) (1998), *Robert Bresson*, Cinematheque Ontario, 1998.
Robert Bresson: Éloge (1997), Milan/Paris, Mazzotta/Cinémathèque française.
Rosenbaum, Jonathan (1998), 'The Last Filmmaker: A Local, Interim Report', in
    James Quandt (ed.), *Robert Bresson*, Cinematheque Ontario, Toronto.

Schofer, Peter (1974), 'Dissolution Into Darkness: Bresson's *Un Condamné à mort s'est échappé*', *Sub-Stance*, no. 9.

Sitney, P. Adams (1998b), 'Cinematography vs. the Cinema: Bresson's Figures', in James Quandt (ed.), *Robert Bresson*, Cinematheque Ontario, Toronto.

Sontag, Susan (1969), 'Spiritual Style in the Films of Robert Bresson', in James Quandt (ed.), *Robert Bresson*, Cinematheque Ontario, Toronto.

Turkle, Sherry (1979), *Psychoanalytic Politics*, London, Burnett Books/André Deutsch.

1

'Bresson before Bresson': *Affaires publiques*, *Les Anges du péché* and *Les Dames du Bois de Boulogne*

Bresson's first film, *Affaires publiques* (1934),[1] is in many ways as unBressonian a work as could be imagined. The director describes it as 'comment dirais-je? pas un "burlesque", pas un "film fantaisiste": la fantaisie, autant que le pittoresque, me fait horreur. Enfin disons: "un comique fou"'.[2] (Estève 1983: 140). The story – picaresque if not picturesque – covers three days in the life of a Ruritanian dictator, played by the clown Beby who was subsequently to be the subject of Jean-Pierre Melville's 1946 documentary *Vingt-quatre heures de la vie d'un clown*. Other roles are taken by Marcel Dalio, best known for his work with Jean Renoir in *La Grande Illusion* and *La Règle du jeu*, and Gilles Margaritis, who plays the pre-Felliniesque clown in Jean Vigo's *L'Atalante*.

Affaires publiques evokes not only Chaplin and Keaton – both among Bresson's favourite film-makers – but also the Vigo of *Zéro de conduite*, the Prévert brothers of *L'Affaire est dans le sac* and the René Clair of *Paris qui dort*. It is episodically amusing, though certain touches such as the inclusion of a black fire-eating fireman have not weathered particularly well, but may seem nowadays largely of curiosity value. Yet it is interesting to note that Roger Leenhardt, reviewing the film in the December 1934 edition of

---

1 This is frequently referred to as *Les Affaires publiques*, but the copy held by the Paris Cinémathèque – so far as I know the only one in existence – shows the title without the article.
2 'what shall I say? – not a "burlesque", nor a "fantasy film": I loathe fantasy as much as the picturesque. Let's call it a "crazy comedy".'

Esprit, speaks of how 'l'œuvre vaut spirituellement par la loyauté de l'effort dans la pauvreté des moyens et par une absence complète de compromission', while criticising it as 'un peu neutre, gris, sans relief' (*Éloge* 1997: 1).[3] Similar remarks have been made about Bresson's later, most unquestionably 'Bressonian' films, whose flattened-out, two-dimensional quality has indeed been singled out by Paul Schrader as their most distinctively transcendental attribute (Schrader, 1972). Jean Sémolué describes *Les Anges du péché* as 'Bresson avant Bresson. Mais c'est aussi déjà Bresson'.[4] (Sémolué 1993: 31). Leenhardt's remarks suggest that that observation may in some degree be true of *Affaires publiques* too.

Les Anges du péché

Les Anges du péché contains a number of elements from the world of more conventional cinema that were to become progressively rarer in Bresson's work. Its dialogues were scripted, from an idea by Father Bruckberger, by Jean Giraudoux, among France's most prominent dramatists at the time, whose name on the credits attracted a good deal of attention. Bresson was not to use a professional dialogue-writer again after *Les Dames*. The cast includes a number of actors who to a modern audience are probably no more than names, but who at the time had or were acquiring considerable reputations. Renée Faure/Anne-Marie made a number of films for Christian-Jaque, whom she was indeed to marry, but was better known for her work with the Comédie-Française, as was Louis Seigner, who plays the prison governor. Jany Holt/Thérèse was one of the most prominent younger actresses of the 1930s and 1940s, notably for Renoir in *Les Bas-Fonds* and Serge de Poligny in *Le Baron fantôme*. Françoise Ducout's description of her acting ('elle se cabre, griffe, mord jusqu'à l'épuisement'[5] (Ducout 1978: 139))

3 'the work is of spiritual value because of the loyal effort it makes with restricted means and its complete absence of compromise ... [But it is] a little neutral, grey, two-dimensional.'
4 'Bresson before Bresson. But it is also already Bresson.'
5 'she rears, scratches, bites until she is exhausted.'

is no less applicable to Mila Parély/Madeleine's best-known role, her overwrought performance as Geneviève in Renoir's *La Règle du jeu*. Such a style, like the amalgam of *auteur* cinema, *cinéma de qualité* and theatre that houses it, is the antithesis of Bresson's 'modèles', and suggests one major reason why he has long been reluctant to number this film among his 'Bressonian' work. The heavy use of non-diegetic music is another feature that was to dwindle in, and after *Mouchette* disappear entirely from, Bresson's films. The music, which like that for his next two films is by Jean-Jacques Grünenwald, contributes infelicitously to what a French audience might describe as the *sulpicien* quality of some aspects of the film. That adjective derives from the Place Saint-Sulpice on the Left Bank in Paris, which houses a number of shops selling kitschy religious artefacts. Grünenwald's syrupy strings and the suspicious melodiousness of the nuns' choir nowadays seem difficult to take altogether seriously, especially for an Anglo-American audience whose repertoire of cinematic nuns is likely to be headed by Julie Andrews in *The Sound of Music*. The picture is, however, very different in a Catholic culture such as that of France. *Sulpicien* films were extremely popular in the 1930s and 1940s, clearly both encouraging and encouraged by the climate that led to Pétainism; Léon Poirier's *L'Appel du silence* (1936), an edifying 'biopic' of a missionary priest in the Sahara, is among the most egregious examples. Nor should it be forgotten that as recently as 1966 Jacques Rivette's Diderot adaptation, *La Religieuse*, was for a while banned by the French government for its disobliging portrayal of convent life.

Les Anges du péché is set in a convent run by the Sisters of Bethany, a Dominican order founded in 1867 to welcome women newly released from prison. Already one of the great Bressonian leitmotifs reveals itself; five of his feature films – the first, the last *(L'Argent)* and the three consecutive works that can be regarded as making up his 'prison cycle' *(Condamné, Pickpocket* and *Procès)* – are set at least in part within prisons. The film centres on the spiritual conflicts and affinities between Anne-Marie, a young woman from a well-off family who feels called to succour those less fortunate than she, and Thérèse, supposedly the most irredeemable inmate of her prison, where she has been unjustly confined for theft. Anne-Marie, warned on arriving at the convent that she risks being taken for a criminal by the outside world, responds: 'C'est un peu pour cela que je viens', and becomes infatuated with the idea of ministering to Thérèse, whom she assures when visiting her in prison: 'Vos cris ne m'empêcheront pas d'entendre votre vraie souffrance'.[6]

On the day of her release, Thérèse buys a revolver and goes to kill the man whose lies sent her to jail. She takes refuge in the convent, where Anne-Marie's zealous spiritual attentions increasingly exasperate her. A row erupts between Anne-Marie and the other nuns over her treatment of a cat, which she believes to be Beelzebub! When she refuses to do public penance she is expelled from the convent. She goes to pray each night on the tomb of the order's founder, where she is found after a storm and brought back. Her frail health prevents her from pronouncing her vows, which are spoken by Thérèse in her stead. Anne-Marie dies and Thérèse is arrested for murder; one of the nuns says to her as she is taken away, 'A bientôt, ma sœur'.[7]

The above synopsis gives, I hope, a good idea of the perhaps disconcerting balance between religiosity and 'Bresson avant Bresson' that characterises *Les Anges du péché*. The theatricality of Anne-Marie's prayers to the founder, the less than naturalistic staging of her death, the over-tuneful choral singing already referred to, the excessive luminescence of the nuns' habits are unlikely to convince a contemporary audience. Yet the spiritual duel at the heart of the film foreshadows analogous conflicts in the later work (notably between Hélène and Agnès in *Les Dames* and, more pessimistically, between *Une femme douce* and her husband), and the final shot of Thérèse being manacled even as she hears the words that promise her redemption is a striking prefiguration of the ending of *Pickpocket* and Michel's words through the bars: 'O Jeanne, pour aller jusqu'à toi, quel drôle de

6 'That is one reason why I'm here' ... 'Your cries will not keep me from hearing your real suffering.'
7 'We'll see you soon, sister.'

chemin il m'a fallu prendre!'.[8] Even the film's articulation, conventional though it may seem, makes use of ellipses in a way that periodically prefigures the later work, as when Mother Saint-Jean's chiding of Anne-Marie for her insistence that Thérèse should be met on her release from prison is followed by a shot of the Prioress and Anne-Marie preparing to do just that (Pipolo 1998: 197–8).

The film has a painterly quality commented on by René Briot, who compares it to the work of the seventeenth-century portraitist Philippe de Champaigne but goes on to say: 'pour qu'il y ait picturalisme, il faut accorder une valeur en soi à l'image; pour Bresson, celle-ci n'a qu'une valeur d'échange[9] (Briot 1957: 23).[10] The distinction between the painterly and the cinematographic might be described as that between images which have a 'value in themselves' and those which have 'only exchange value', so that Les Anges du péché's specifically cinematographic qualities through which it avoids sanctimoniousness and accedes to an 'exchange value', of images and souls alike, may be better sought in its drawing on two sets of genre conventions – those of on the one hand documentary, on the other film noir. Bresson from Journal onwards works to all intents and purposes outside genre, with the exception of those parts of Pickpocket and the inserts in Le Diable probablement that are close to the documentary. The historical caption that opens Les Anges du péché, and the intentness with which the film, largely studio-shot though it is, recreates the authentic rituals of convent life, from communal manual work to the correction fraternelle in which each sister is entitled to ask the others for a frank spiritual appraisal, bring it closer to the documentary than anything else in Bresson's work. Yet the appearance of documentary realism often seems there only to be shattered by the outbreak of spiritual – sometimes actual – violence, most strikingly in the sequence where Thérèse flings the soup trolley down the prison stairs.

8 'Oh Jeanne, to come to you, what a strange path I had to travel!'
9 'for there to be pictorialism, the image needs to be granted a value in itself; but for Bresson, it has only exchange value.'
10 Kline gives a Saussurean reading of Bresson's 'language of images', stressing like Briot the images' exchange value rather than any intrinsic quality they may have (Kline 1992: 153-4).

The *noir* elements – less incongruous than they might sound in what is after all a battle between good and evil – figure in the sequences outside the convent – two nuns walking down an archetypally mean night-time street near the prison,[11] Thérèse, for one shot at least a *femme fatale*, pulling the gun on her (presumed) former lover, even the laconic though scarcely very penetrating conversations between the detectives in the police station. 'French *noir*' was a highly popular genre in the 1930s and 1940s (Renoir's *La Nuit du carrefour*, Carné's *Le Quai des brumes*, Clouzot's *Le Corbeau* are among the outstanding examples), so that it is not surprising that a débutant director should draw upon its conventions. Bresson was soon to find other, more inwardly focused ways of writing ethical and spiritual conflict.

The film was favourably received on its release, lauded among others by Sacha Guitry for whom '[c]'est bien mieux que du cinéma'[12] (Guitry 1997: 13), and – in one of his earliest published writings – Roland Barthes. Barthes displays a characteristic sensitivity to the film's ethical ambiguities ('tout le long du film, on a senti que le Bien n'était pas tellement séparé du Mal' (Barthes 1997: 16)),[13] and sees the ending as rescued from tragedy only by Father Bruckberger's Dominican view of redemption and, by implication, Bresson's scopophilia ('on sait en quelle estime – pour des motifs différents – les Dominicains et les cinéastes tiennent le spectacle d'une belle mort' (Barthes 1997: 17)).[14] It is a later Barthes, associated with perversity and *jouissance*, that is evoked by Louis Skorecki in his *Libération* piece 'Un Bresson sexuel', which views Anne-Marie's destruction of her family photographs as analogous to Bresson's desire to destroy the conventions of the *cinéma de qualité* and describes the sequence where the rain beats down on Anne-Marie's face as 'la seule fois où Bresson a filmé hard'.[15] On this reading, Anne-Marie dies because she has achieved

11 Pipolo sees this sequence as evocative of an underground Resistance operation (Pipolo 1998: 202).
12 'it is much better than cinema.'
13 'throughout the film, we have felt that Good was not so far removed from Evil.'
14 'we know how highly, for different reasons, Dominicans and film-makers regard the sight of a good death.'
15 'the only time Bresson has filmed hard-core.'

the status to which nuns aspire, that of bride of Christ, only too successfully; 'de ce foutre de Dieu, elle a joui à mort'[16] (Skorecki 1984). The slightly self-conscious Sadeo–Bataillesque tone of this reading should not blind us to the presence, in this sequence and perhaps also in the waterfall scene in Les Dames, of a harsh, penetrative, sexualised sensuality that is pared away in much of the later work. Bresson's sadistic eroticism will henceforth find more ascetic ways of inscribing itself.

For a contemporary public, the most difficult aspect of Les Anges du péché is likely to be the theological concepts and discourses in which it abounds. 'C'est quand le monde prend la forme d'une feuille de papier qu'il pèse sur nous de tout son poids',[17] that line from the film could stand as an epigraph for the logocentrism fundamental to Bresson's Catholicism, instanced throughout his work by the aphoristic, citational quality of so much of the dialogue. The term 'dialogue', indeed, is often misleading, implying as it may do a merging or interplay between interlocutors which might appear to undermine the otherness so essential throughout Bresson. Lacan's observation on the duality inherent in any relationship with the other is applicable to Bresson's work right from Les Anges du péché: 'le sujet se trouve inclus dans un rapport duel, et donc ambigu, avec l'autre comme tel dans cette sorte de ou bien ou bien qui est fondamental de cette relation duelle'[18] (Saint-Drôme 1994: 72). It is that 'ou bien ou bien', that 'either-or', that subtends the spiritual duel between Thérèse and the other – Anne-Marie – who all but bids to take her over, a duel clearly understood by the prioress when having charged Thérèse to watch over the dying Anne-Marie she explains: 'Nous n'avons pas le droit de les séparer au moment où devient évident le jeu qui se joue entre elles'.[19] That 'jeu', which takes the

16 'she has carried her *jouissance* of God's spunk unto death.'
17 'It is when the world takes the form of a sheet of paper that it weighs most fully upon us.'
18 'the subject is included in a dual, and thus ambiguous, relationship with the other as such in that kind of "either–or" which forms the basis of that dual relation.'
19 'We have no right to separate them just as the game being played out between them is becoming obvious.'

form above all of a play of looks between the two women, is no sport but quite literally an endgame of (eternal) life and death between two different forms of pride – Anne-Marie's colonising spiritual fervour and Thérèse's angry resistance, grounded doubtless in an awareness that she has entered the convent to flee human justice rather than to seek that of God. A fundamental Catholic concept here is that of the transferability of merit and, conversely, of guilt, concentrated metonymically in Christ's death on the Cross in which he took upon himself the burden of all the wrongs of humanity. I call this 'Catholic' rather than 'Christian' because the Protestant tradition places much greater stress on each individual's responsibility for him/herself, tending to play down the transindividual dimension represented by the communion of saints of which religious orders are a microcosm. In this light, Anne-Marie's expulsion from the convent is more than the act of authoritarian spite it may appear; her stubborn assertion of her individuality performatively breaks with the communion of saints, just as Thérèse's bad faith in joining the order for the wrong reason means that she has never genuinely been part of it. Anne-Marie's virtual death from exposure on the founder's grave – a return to the Father indeed – produces within her the 'void' which for Simone Weil is necessary for grace to enter,[20] and when that grace enters its action is manifold, incorporating Thérèse into the communion of saints for the first time as well as bringing Anne-Marie back within it. Thérèse's pronouncing of Anne-Marie's vows is thus much more than a surrogate exercise, nor is it the 'victory' of Anne-Marie that Thérèse's speaking on behalf of Anne-Marie ('Moi, sœur Anne-Marie') might suggest. Such a reading would, in a Pascalian perspective not unfamiliar to Lacan too, be grounded in the law and not in grace, for 'la loi obligeait à ce qu'elle ne donnait pas. La grâce donne ce à quoi elle oblige' (Pascal [1670] 1976: 192).[21] For Thérèse and Anne-Marie, the 'jeu qui se joue entre elles' has culminated, not in the triumph of the law and the abolition of two recalcitrant individualities, but in that of grace and their transcendental fusion.

20 See above, p. x.
21 'the law made obligatory what it did not give. Grace gives what it makes obligatory.'

It may seem perverse to describe a film in which one central character dies prematurely and another is carted off to prison as having a happy ending, but in the Bressonian perspective that is an accurate description of *Les Anges du péché*. If Thérèse prefigures *Pickpocket*'s Michel, Anne-Marie at the end, transcending herself through self-abnegation and thus in a sense asserting herself far more truly than before, evokes the country priest in *Journal*. For all the glossiness of the photography, the obtrusiveness of the music, the evident *acting* of the actors, *Les Anges du péché* is indeed, to reprise Sémolué, 'déjà Bresson'.

Les Dames du Bois de Boulogne

Bresson's second feature was shot between May 1944 and February 1945 – a much longer period than it would normally have taken owing to the severely restricted electricity supply in the final years of the war, which led to an interruption of filming for almost six months and came close to causing the film to be abandoned. Paul Guth's *Autour des Dames du Bois de Boulogne* is an absorbing account of wartime filming and its frustrations, in which the author describes one of the scenes between the three female protagonists as 'le genre de scène que chérissent les fervents du théâtre filmé, qu'abhorrent les cinéastes purs: longs dialogues, caméra promenée d'un visage à l'autre'.[22] (Guth 1945: 118–19). As unBressonian a tableau as one could imagine, at first sight; and yet *Les Dames* seems to me to conform still more than the earlier film to Sémolué's description of *Les Anges du péché* as 'Bresson avant Bresson'.

The film is a contemporary adaptation of an episode from Diderot's picaresque eighteenth-century novel *Jacques le fataliste*, which tells how a rejected woman's attempted revenge upon and humiliation of her former lover misfires and, not without problems, procures his happiness. If for Diderot, or at least for the hostess who narrates this story, 'il n'y a que les femmes qui sachent

---

22 'this is the kind of scene beloved of fans of filmed theatre but abhorred by pure cineastes: long dialogues, with the camera moving from one face to another.'

aimer; les hommes n'y entendent rien' (Diderot [1796] 1962: 599),[23] Bresson's film is far less categorical, largely because the drama is situated on the interior, even spiritual, rather than on the social level. Diderot's Marquis des Arcis, trapped into marrying a former *demimondaine*, absents himself from Paris for three years with his wife when he discovers the truth; no such purging of society's contempt is required of Bresson's Jean, whose love in the final sequence may call his dying wife Agnès back to life.

The similarities and divergences between the Diderot novel and the Bresson film are helpfully condensed by Jean Sémolué in the earlier of his two books on Bresson. For Sémolué, 'dans une perspective dramatique, celle de Diderot, ce qui compte, c'est l'acte; dans une perspective tragique, celle de Bresson, ce sont les effets de l'acte sur l'âme'[24] (Sémolué 1959: 47). This suggests one important way in which *Les Dames* is unmistakably a Bressonian film, though with a screenplay by Cocteau and established actors in the lead roles it is obvious that in many respects it is close to filmed theatre. Élina Labourdette (Agnès) was to go on to a modestly successful career in flirtatious comic roles, as for Jacques Becker in *Édouard et Caroline*, before in a sense reprising her role from *Les Dames* in Demy's *Lola*, where a youthful photograph of her character (Madame Desnoyers) is actually taken from *Les Dames*. Maria Casarès (Hélène), most prominent as a stage actress, had become known to a cinema audience in the role of Nathalie in Carné's *Les Enfants du paradis* (released shortly before *Les Dames*), and was to go on to the apogee of 'son propre mythe de tragédienne'[25] (Passek 1987: 72) for Cocteau in *Orphée*. Françoise Ducout assimilates the three central female actresses to archetypes common in the cinema of the 1940s – Labourdette the young *ingénue*, Casarès the *femme fatale*, Lucienne Bogaert the mother – but signals their distance from that world by describing them as 'déjà femmes d'aujourd'hui'[26] (Ducourt 1978: 140).

23 'women are the only ones who know how to love; men understand nothing about it.'
24 'in a dramatic perspective (Diderot's), what counts is the act; in a tragic perspective (Bresson's), what counts is the effects of the act upon the soul.'
25 'her own myth as a tragedian.'
26 'already women of today.'

Paul Bernard, in the role of Jean, is by common consent the film's weakest link. For the much underrated Jean Grémillon he had given a far more convincing performance in a not radically dissimilar role as the disturbed, indeed homicidal, lord of the manor in *Lumière d'été*, yet for Bresson, whose first choice for the role had been Alain Cuny, he appears chilly and stilted to a degree that is intensified by on the one hand Labourdette's freshness, on the other Casarès's passion. The widespread criticism his performance attracted may have influenced Bresson's subsequent decision to abjure professional actors.

It was doubtless thanks to Cocteau's participation and the comparatively star-studded cast that the film opened at the Rex – Paris's largest cinema, on the *grands boulevards*, and since its opening the first port of call for big-screen spectaculars. A more incongruous spot to screen a Bresson film it would be hard to imagine. Yet according to Jacques Becker: 'Le grand public a compris Bresson, je le sais, et j'ai pu m'en assurer dans une grande salle des Boulevards où quelque trois mille spectateurs suivaient ce film dans un silence attentif'[27] (*Hommage* 1997: 20). A discordant note was, however, struck by Raymond Queneau, for whom it was the worst film of its year (Queneau 1945). Bresson's subsequent evolution – his 'becoming Bresson', in an ultra-auteurist perspective – was to take him away from a type of cinema, under-stood both as genre and as venue, to which *Les Dames*, though only his second feature, marks his farewell.

Les Dames tells how Hélène, forewarned by a friend that Jean is tiring of her, pretends to him that she has tired of him ('mon cœur se détache de vous'),[28] only for this bluff to be called by Jean's admission of relief. She swears vengeance over the sound of tap-dancing – an extraordinary sound–image dislocation reintegrated by the sight immediately afterwards of Agnès dancing in a night-club. Élina Labourdette's expression of innocence is belied by her garb, which would have been deemed immodestly revealing for a

27 'The public has understood Bresson, I know, and I had the proof of this in a large Boulevard cinema in which some three thousand spectators followed the film in attentive silence.'
28 'my heart is detaching itself from you.'

'respectable' woman of the time. Conversations reveal that she and her mother, old friends of Hélène's, have fallen on hard times financially and that Agnès is reduced to periodic sleeping with her admirers to pay the bills. Hélène sets Agnès and her mother up in a flat and arranges a meeting between them and Jean by the waterfall in the Bois de Boulogne – Paris's largest park, with an appropriately dubious reputation. Jean begins to fall in love with Agnès, who out of shame at first flees his advances; he refuses to read the letter in which she confesses her status. Hélène through her insistence engineers a grand wedding, at the end of which she tells Jean: 'Vous avez épousé une grue'.[29] Agnès, who has a weak heart, has three fainting fits. Jean arrives at her bedside, declares his love and pleads with her to stay. The film ends on her words: 'Je reste'.[30] Godard, in a characteristically coat-trailing gesture, invoked her previous line, 'Je lutte',[31] to claim that Les Dames was 'the "only" film of the French Resistance' (Rosenbaum 1998: 22), bestowing upon it an otherwise unwarranted kinship with Carné's Les Visiteurs du soir of two years before.

Les Dames, as the above outline suggests, has more in common with Les Anges du péché than its very different setting might suggest. The only sunlit scene is the first meeting beside the waterfall, and the looming black cars and frequent rain evoke the noir aspects of the earlier film. Implausible sojourns at death's door close both narratives, though human love triumphs in calling Agnès back to life in Les Dames rather than divine love asserting itself in death as in Les Anges du péché. Both films have at their heart the rivalry between two women one of whom seeks to manipulate the other with results very different from those she had planned (had Paul Bernard's performance been less lacklustre this aspect of Les Dames would doubtless not have been quite so prominent). Agnès, indeed, as her name (= 'lamb') suggests, can be seen as the first of the femmes douces who abound in Bresson's work well before the film of that name, and whose meekness, at once stimulatingly and disconcertingly in a gender

29 'You have married a tart.'
30 'I'll stay.'
31 'I'm battling.'

perspective, is the source of their strength, belying Houston and Kinder's simplistic assertion of the 'abject helplessness of the [female] victims' in Bresson's later *œuvre* (Houston and Kinder 1980: 216). Yet she is not above stubbing out an over-attentive admirer's cigarette in his face – the kind of gesture more often associated with men in *film noir* (James Cagney's grapefruit in Mae Clarke's face in Wellman's *The Public Enemy* and Lee Marvin's scalding of Gloria Grahame in Lang's *The Big Heat* are the two most notorious examples). *Noir* too is the belted raincoat – a kind of trenchcoat *manqué* – she invariably wears in the outdoor scenes, contrasting with Hélène's cornucopian elegance. Unfavourable critical comments on the (im)plausibility of this seem to me to miss the point twice over; if Agnès is reduced to part-time prostitution to keep herself and her mother it is all too likely that she will be able to afford only one raincoat, and in any event sartorial *vraisemblance* has never been a major concern of Bresson's, as both *Pickpocket* and *Le Procès* will show.

Maria Casarès is the only full-blown *femme fatale* in Bresson's work, her manipulative sultriness and brooding gaze more than a match for her French or American counterparts (Ginette Leclerc, Viviane Romance, Bette Davis) and contributing as much as the night-time ambiance to the film's *noir* affiliation. How magnificent she would have been as Madame de Merteuil in an adaptation of Laclos's *Les Liaisons dangereuses*! *Les Dames* is certainly the most worldly of Bresson's films, its milieu of well-heeled disaffection closer to Antonioni than to its director's later work. Yet to view it purely as a bourgeois melodrama would be to amputate one of its most important dimensions, suggested by André Bazin in '*Le Journal d'un curé de campagne* et la stylistique de Robert Bresson':

> Dans *Les Dames du bois de Boulogne*, Bresson a spéculé sur le dépaysement d'un conte réaliste dans un autre contexte réaliste. Le résultat, c'est que les réalismes se détruisent l'un l'autre, les passions se dégagent de la chrysalide des caractères, l'action des alibis de l'intrigue, et la tragédie des oripeaux du drame. Il n'a fallu que le bruit d'un essuie-glace d'automobile sur un texte de Diderot pour en faire un dialogue racinien.[32] (Bazin 1985: 112)

32 'In *Les Dames*, Bresson speculated on the displacement of a realist tale into

Diderot transposed into a contemporary setting, in other words, gives us not the eighteenth century in modern dress but the classical tragedy of the seventeenth – a tragedy grounded in the Jansenism we have already seen to be characteristic of Bresson. The windscreen-wiper sound, in the opening sequence where Hélène is returning from the theatre by taxi with her confidant Jacques, is premonitory of the raking of the leaves in the pivotal scene of *Journal*, between the priest and the Countess, or of the clicking of the racecourse turnstiles in *Pickpocket* – both suggestive of mechanisms of grace and its apparent opposite beyond the reach of conscious human agency. Henri Agel likewise detects a parallel between *Les Dames* and the later film in their non-naturalistic, even deconstructive, use of language ('Déjà, avec *Les Dames*, la parole introduisait un élément d'insolite, à dessein, souvent faux, révélant ainsi que l'essentiel se jouait à l'envers du langage' (Agel 1954: 38)).[33] Cocteau's deployment of language as an ironic commentary not only on the action, but on itself (Hélène to the lovelorn Jean: 'Vous passez votre vie à attendre, dans des escaliers, des grottes, des gares'[34] – one example among a myriad) plays an important part in this, and will be a characteristic of the dialogues Bresson himself was to write from *Journal* onwards. The non-transparency of language is most strikingly figured when, in a despairing attempt to get Jean to read the letter in which she confesses to her past life, Agnès slips it under the wipers of his car, from which it immediately blows back to her. 'The wind bloweth where it listeth', indeed – the original working title ('Le vent souffle où il veut') for *Un condamné*; the shot also foreshadows the note from Jeanne that Michel will find a day late in *Pickpocket*. For Bresson as for Lacan, 'une lettre arrive

another realist context. The result is that the two realisms destroy each other, the passions emerging from the characters' chrysalises as the action does from the alibis of the plot and tragedy from the trappings of drama. All that was needed was the sound of a windscreen-wiper over a Diderot text to make a Racinian dialogue.'
33 'Already in *Les Dames* the dialogues intentionally introduced an element of the unwonted, often a false one, thereby revealing that the essence of the film was situated on the other side of language.'
34 'You spend your life waiting, in stairways, caves, stations.'

toujours à destination' (Lacan 1966: 53),[35] but that destin(y)ation is
not necessarily – even necessarily not – that consciously willed by
the sender, for psychoanalyst and Jansenist alike. 'Les écrits
emportent au vent les traites en blanc d'une cavalerie folle' (Lacan
1966: 37),[36] and in so doing paradoxically ensure that those bills
will be paid in full – by Agnès on the brink of death, by Hélène
thwarted *in extremis* of her revenge and – perhaps most inter-
estingly despite Paul Bernard's insipidity – by Jean himself.

The sadistic is conventionally associated with the male, and the
masochistic, as Bresson's numerous *femmes douces* suggest, with
the female. Yet this distribution is often enough reversed in his
work to be called into question. The country priest, Michel in *Pickpocket*, Jacques in *Les Dames du Bois de Boulogne* all display evident
masochistic qualities. Hélène's willingness to ruin three lives in
pursuit of revenge is imbued by Maria Casarès with distinctly
sadistic qualities, though if to those lives we add a possible fourth
– her own – masochism reinscribes itself. The ambivalence of this
impression is strengthened by the fact that we see nothing of her
after her gloating announcement to Jean through the window of
his car. Feminist theology has often perceived the Annunciation –
the penetration of the Virgin Mary's ear by the phallogocentric
word of the angel – as an invasive or violative act.[37] This view
doubtless underpins Dominique Païni's reading of *Les Dames* as a
mise en scène , via montage, of the Angel Gabriel's proclamation to
Mary ('[la] transformation d'un motif pictural incontestablement
chargé de temporalité, en une dramaturgie qui se développe, par
définition, dans la durée' (Païni 1993: 63)).[38] The Heideggerian
temporalities here are perhaps of less interest than the question of
how the respective roles of Gabriel and Mary are filled. If the
'inquiétante étrangeté'[39] (Païni 1993: 64) of Hélène – cousin to the

35 'a letter always reaches its destination.'
36 'Writings carry away on the wind the blank bills of exchange of a crazed cavalry.'
37 The wimple was worn in the Middle Ages because Christ was popularly believed
     to have been born through Mary's ear, which thus became a potential erogenous
     zone.
38 '[the] transformation of a pictorial motif undoubtedly charged with temporality
     into a drama which by definition unfolds in duration.'
39 '[the] disturbing strangeness.'

Freudian *Unheimliche*/uncanny? – seems to make of her the (bad) angel in Bresson's rewriting, thereby in part inverting the gender distribution of the original, there are two recipients of her announcements – three if we count Agnès's mother, so supine and ineffectual that it would be easy to forget about her (examples of good parenting in Bresson, we shall see, are thin on the ground). Agnès is informed of the changed life Hélène is to bestow upon her, and despite her misgivings has little choice but to comply. Yet the 'Annunciation' on which the entire film hinges, splendidly Proustian in its choice of vocabulary, is Hélène's proclamation to Jean (something of a Swann *manqué*?): 'Vous avez épousé une grue'. Plausibility – admittedly often not a major consideration in Bresson – may lead us to think that a man so worldly-wise might have had suspicions about Agnes' past, and his strenuous refusal to read her confession strongly suggests that this may well be so. Hearing, notably in the Annunciation and its variants, can be perceived as a more passive, so to speak feminised way of receiving tidings than reading, which suggests one way in which Jean's – unwitting – postponement of the revelation until after the wedding, when it is too late, smacks of a masochistic acquiescence in his own castration. Not only does Jean hear the truth about Agnès rather than reading it, he does so from the lips of one driven by the desire to destroy him rather than anything so noble as honesty.

Yet that acquiescence, that submission, like in a far more overtly spiritualised manner the country priest's, does not destroy Jean, but redeems him, and much as in *Les Anges du péché* that redemption is a twofold one. The prioress's words in the earlier film – 'Nous n'avons pas le droit de les séparer au moment où devient évident le jeu qui se joue entre elles' – could if 'elles' were replaced by 'eux' apply to the ending of *Les Dames*. Two characters who have both submitted to the tyrannical 'annunciations' of Hélène finally find themselves brought closer and strengthened by that submission, while their 'bad angel' is less discomfited than simply abolished, expunged from the action of the film in a manner no less sadistic for being discreet once she has fulfilled her role. Submissive femininity, *Les Dames* may be suggesting, is not the exclusive property of the feminine gender.

The transferability of merit that suffuses *Les Anges du péché* and *Les Dames* alike, the sado-masochistic dynamics of their plots and *mise en scène*, the narrative ellipses they periodically practice all entitle us to see them as at least in part genuinely Bressonian films. Hélène's disappearance from the film after her 'annunciation' is less dramatic, but no less unexplained, than Marie's in *Balthazar* twenty and more years later. In this sense, and despite the use of well-known actors and the specially written music (of which only the latter was to survive, and for one more film only), *Les Anges du péché* and *Les Dames* clearly announce Bresson as an *auteur* in the sense in which Geoffrey Nowell-Smith understands the term:

> One essential corollary of the theory as it has been developed is the discovery that the defining characteristics of an author's work are not necessarily those which are most readily apparent. The purpose of criticism thus becomes to uncover behind the superficial contrasts of subject and treatment a hard core of basic and often recondite motifs. (Wollen 1970: 80)

Auteurism is a critical theory once but no longer hegemonic, as the foreword to this series explicitly acknowledges. The past twenty or so years have seen an erosion of the traditional boundaries between art-house and commercial cinema, accompanied by a largely gender-influenced upsurge of interest in star studies and a 'new historicist' approach focusing on cinema as an industry, which between them have whittled away the importance of *auteur* theory. If there is one director in post-war French cinema to whom it remains overwhelmingly applicable, however, that director is Bresson. The comparative meagreness of his output, his refusal of actors and thus of the star system, the theological or at least transcendental underpinnings that are a constant of his work along with its insistent materiality, all help to make him one of the very few unquestioned *auteurs* of his time. That authorship, we have seen, is present even in films he now at least partially disowns; it is to flourish at once more fully and more ascetically in his work from *Journal* onwards.

References

Agel, Henri (1954), *Le Cinéma et le sacré*, Paris, Cerf.

Barthes, Roland (1997), '*Les Anges du péché*', in *Robert Bresson: Éloge*, Milan/Paris, Mazzotta/Cinémathèque française.

Bazin, André (1985), *Qu'est-ce que le cinéma?* Paris, Cerf.

Becker, Jacques (1997), 'Les Dames du bois de Boulogne', in *Robert Bresson: Éloge*, Milan/Paris, Mazzotta/Cinémathèque française.

Briot, René (1957), *Robert Bresson*, Paris, Cerf.

Diderot, Denis ([1796] 1962), *Œuvres romanesques*, Paris, Garnier.

Ducout, Françoise (1978), *Séductrices du cinéma français*, Paris, Henri Veyrier.

Estève, Michel (1983), *Robert Bresson: la passion du cinématographe*, Paris, Albatros.

Guitry, Sacha (1997), 'Les Anges du péché', in *Robert Bresson: Éloge*, Milan/Paris, Mazzotta/Cinémathèque française.

Guth, Paul (1989), *Autour des 'Dames du bois de Boulogne'*, Paris, Ramsay.

Houston, Beverley and Kinder, Marsha (1980), *Self and Cinema – A Transformalist Perspective*, Pleasantville, Redgrave.

Kline, T. Jefferson (1992), *Screening the Text: Intertextuality in French New Wave Cinema*, Baltimore, Johns Hopkins University Press.

Lacan, Jacques (1966), *Écrits I*, Paris, Seuil.

Leenhardt, Roger (1997), 'Les Affaires publiques', in *Robert Bresson: Éloge*, Milan/Paris, Mazzotta/Cinémathèque française.

Païni, Dominique (1993), 'Le Dispositif annonciatif comme montage', in Barthélémy Amengual (ed.), *Études cinématographiques*, no. 153–5.

Pascal, Blaise ([1670] 1976), *Pensées*, Paris, GF-Flammarion.

Passek, Jean-Loup (1987), *Dictionaire du cinéma français*, Paris, Larouse.

Pipolo, Tony (1998), 'Rules of the Game: On Bresson's *Les Anges du péché*', in James Quandt (ed.), *Robert Bresson*, Cinematheque Ontario, Toronto.

Rosenbaum, Jonathan (1998), 'The Last Filmmaker: A Local, Interim Report', in James Quandt (ed.), *Robert Bresson*, Cinematheque Ontario, Toronto.

Saint-Drôme, Oreste (1994), *Dictionnaire inespéré de 55 termes visités par Jacques Lacan*, Paris, Seuil.

Schrader, Paul (1972), *Transcendental Style in Film: Ozu, Bresson, Dreyer*, Los Angeles/London, University of California Press.

Sémolué, Jean (1959), *Robert Bresson*, Paris, Éditions Universitaires.

Sémolué, Jean (1993), *Bresson ou l'acte pur des métamorphoses*, Paris, Flammarion.

Skorecki, Louis (1984), 'Un Bresson sexuel', *Libération*, 18 December.

Wollen, Peter (1970), *Signs and Meaning in the Cinema*, London, Thames & Hudson/BFI.

2

Journal d'un curé de campagne

In 1947, Bresson went to Rome to work on a screenplay of the life of St Ignatius Loyola, founder of the Jesuits, which was never to be filmed. This renewal of his interest in the religious life bore fruit in *Journal d'un curé de campagne* of 1951, adapted from the celebrated novel by Georges Bernanos. Almost entirely faithful to the novel, Bresson's film is nevertheless radically different from it – more introspective, less sensual, far less concerned with the broader canvas of the priest's relationships with his parishioners. The forty-five minutes of footage that were cut at the editing stage largely showed the priest in that wider context (for example, saying Mass). Of these scenes, Bresson commented that they 'd'elles-mêmes se sont refusées à entrer dans la composition du film. M'y obstiner, ç'eût été mettre le film tout entier en danger de mort'[1] (*Éloge* 1997: 86). Marie-Claire Ropars-Wuillemier observes that 'ainsi délivré de ses éléments spectaculaires, l'espace devient disponible pour suggérer non plus le contenu d'une vision, mais bien la temporalité d'un regard'[2] (Ropars-Wuillemier 1970: 101), a remark true of Bresson in general but perhaps of his Bernanos adaptations in particular.

Bresson's was not the first adaptation of the Bernanos novel to have been proposed for the cinema. Jean Aurenche and Pierre

---

1 '[they] refused of themselves to form part of the composition of the film. To have insisted on them would have been to put the entire film in danger of death.'
2 'thus relieved of its spectacular elements, space becomes available to suggest no longer the content of a vision, but the temporality of a gaze.'

Bost, the screenwriting duo who dominated the *cinéma de qualité* and were duly execrated by the New Wave, had prepared an adaptation in which the priest's dying words, instead of the 'tout est grâce'[3] of Bernanos and then Bresson, were to have been: 'Quand on est mort, tout est mort, tout est mort'.[4] A more flagrant distortion of the original it would be difficult to imagine. Aurenche and Bost had collaborated five years before the Bresson film on Jean Delannoy's adaptation of André Gide's *La Symphonie pastorale*, about a Protestant pastor's ultimately fatal infatuation with a blind girl in his charge, whose melodramatic acting and laboured studio filming put it at the antipodes to Bresson's work. Dudley Andrew describes the Delannoy film as 'performed by the French Quality Orchestra' (Andrew 1984: 98); the chamber ambiance of Bresson's filming, increasingly apparent through his work, inscribes itself in *Journal* not only in contrast to Bernanos's sensual canvas, but in opposition to the *cinéma de qualité* vision.

The film was shot and edited on location in the northern French village of Équirre (near Bernanos's birthplace). For the part of the priest, Bresson eliminated all non-believers before selecting Claude Laydu, who spent time meditating in Normandy before filming, wore a real priest's cassock during shooting and underate to achieve a suitably pinched mien. Such devices may seem evocative of Method acting and Lee Strasberg's Actors' Studio, but the psychological realism of a Marlon Brando or a James Dean is a world away from the spiritual rigour of Bresson's Laydu. Armand Guibert, who plays the *curé* of Torcy, was a psychiatrist and according to some sources at least Bresson's analyst (though he claimed never to have been in analysis), while Nicole Ladmiral (Chantal) had delivered some of the commentary to Franju's documentary *Le Sang des bêtes* of 1949. She is assimilated by Burch and Sellier to 'la longue cohorte de "garces maléfiques" que produit le cinéma français d'après-guerre'[5] (Burch and Sellier 1996: 288) – a remark that reminds us at once of how *Journal* retains links with an earlier cinema and of how

3 'all is grace.'
4 'When you are dead, everything is dead, everything is dead.'
5 'The long line of "maleficent bitches" of postwar French cinema.'

radically Bresson was taking his distance from it. The 'garces' in question, from Viviane Romance in Duvivier's *La Belle Équipe* of 1936 through to Danièle Delorme in the same director's *Voici le temps des assassins* twenty years later, manipulate men sexually to get their hands on their money. Chantal's malevolence, like her acting (if that is the word), is of a quite different, materially disinterested order.

None of the *modèles*, as it now seems appropriate to call them, of *Journal* was to go on to a major cinematic career. Nicole Ladmiral, after working in journalism, did what her character in the film threatens to do and committed suicide in 1958, while Claude Laydu became a children's television presenter. The film, which won the Prix Louis Delluc, was unsurprisingly better received on its release by Catholic than by non- or anti-Catholic critics, despite being banned in Portugal. It was praised by Julien Green and François Mauriac, the latter of whom, in *Le Figaro*, asked: 'Si l'écran tendu devant la foule était ce linge qui a essuyé une seule fois la sueur et le sang de l'humanité et qui se propose en vain à nos yeux aveugles, à nos cœurs fermés?'[6] (*Éloge* 1997: 23) – a question that derives much of its force from the analogy between Séraphita Dumouchel as she wipes the barely conscious priest's face and the Veronica of the Passion. For the rambunctiously anti-clerical Ado Kyrou in *L'Age du cinéma*, on the other hand, the film was merely destined to win 'les nombreuses louanges des punaises de sacristie, des jeunes curés boutonneux et des ennemis, conscients ou non, déclarés ou non, du cinéma'[7] (Droguet 1966: 87).

If the film speaks eloquently and powerfully to non-believers, as despite Kyrou it clearly often does, this is in large part due to formal properties indissociable from what would conventionally be described as its 'plot', and distilled by André Bazin in his remarkable essay '*Le Journal d'un curé de campagne* et la stylistique

6 'What if the screen held up before the crowd were the cloth that once and once only wiped away humanity's sweat and blood and that vainly offers itself to our blind eyes, our closed hearts?'
7 'Widespread praise from bigoted old maids, spotty young priests and enemies, whether or not conscious, of the cinema.'

de Robert Bresson'. Chief among these is the film's foregrounding of the process of writing. We see the priest's hand (in reality Bresson's) in close-up writing his diary as we hear Laydu's voice reading the lines aloud – a doubling-up of the action which becomes a tripling-up when we witness what has been described. Gilles Deleuze has spoken of 'la célèbre voix bressonienne, la voix du "modèle" ... où le personnage parle comme s'il écoutait ses propres paroles rapportées par un autre, pour atteindre à une *littéralité* de la voix, la couper de toute résonance directe, et lui faire produire un discours indirect libre'[8] (Deleuze 1985: 315). This account fits the voice-over in *Journal* well enough for Laydu to be considered the first of Bresson's 'modèles', and in one way at least the most audacious, for the 'autre' to whom he is as if listening is surely none other than God.

Whether or not we take that step from the formal to the theological – a step to which the whole film might seem an invitation – the work's systematic recursiveness makes a summary of the plot, along the lines I here try to provide, unusually difficult, for the scenes we witness are by the very fact of having been written down situated in the past rather than in the more normal cinematic present, and their transcription – as might be said their transcoding from material action to spiritual reflection – forms an integral part of them.

In the opening sequence we see the priest writing and hear him saying: 'Je ne crois rien faire de mal en notant ici, au jour le jour, avec une franchise absolue, les très humbles, les insignifiants secrets d'une vie d'ailleurs sans mystère'[9] (Bernanos 1974: 35). This statement is of course inaccurate; the priest's humdrum life in an unlovely and ungrateful parish is pervaded by that greatest of all mysteries that is grace, and the 'jotting down' that he at once trivialises and seeks to justify is to prove, in a properly

---

8 'The famous Bressonian voice, the voice of the "model" ... in which the characters speak as if they were listening to their own words reported by somebody else, to attain a *literalness* of the voice, cutting off any direct resonance and causing it to produce indirect free speech.'

9 'I don't think I am doing wrong in jotting down, day by day, without hiding anything, the very humble and insignificant secrets of a life quite without mystery.'

sacramental sense, that grace's agent. The music, less glutinous than in the previous two films, is still heavier than in Bresson's subsequent work, sounding at times oddly like parts of the slow movement from Mahler's Fifth Symphony made popular by Visconti's *Death in Venice* – a film as unlike Bresson's in every other respect as could be imagined. The first outdoor sequence shows us the count and his daughter's governess furtively embracing, viewed through the grille of the château's gates – the third, along with the priest's anguished face and the diary, of the visual constants that for René Briot structure the film (Briot 1957: 48). We then see the priest, in his presbytery, drinking the red wine that provides the only nourishment he can take – by realist standards of plausibility an unlikely state of affairs, but not difficult to read as a sacramental analogy. He is visited by the brusque and rubicund *curé* of Torcy, the neighbouring parish, whose exhortation 'Faites de l'ordre à longueur du jour'[10] may appear inappositely peremptory if we do not bear in mind that the *curé* of Torcy is a complement to Laydu's priest rather than an alternative or even oppositional exemplar of the vocation. Catholic theology views the Church, like the Godhead, as threefold, and the Church Triumphant of eternity to which the priest accedes through his death at the end could not exist without its earthly counterparts the Church Suffering and the Church Militant, represented by Laydu's priest and the *curé* of Torcy respectively.

The priest is taunted by his brightest catechism pupil, Séraphita Dumouchel, who tells him what lovely eyes he has while her classmates listen giggling outside the door. Later, returning a bag Séraphita has intentionally dropped at his feet, he is angrily received by her mother; his capacity to disturb seems to apply with particular force to the female gender, in accord with the sexual dynamics that are at work even in this, along with *Un condamné* the least overtly sexualised of Bresson's films. His nights are tortured by the stomach cancer that is to claim his life, but also by the literally excruciating burden of responsibility he has taken on for the parish and every soul within it. The threefold solitude that Paul

---

10 'Create order the whole day long.'

Schrader, following Sémolué, identifies within the film – another trinitarian structure of grace at work – is precisely that, one solitude in three ('(1) sickness : the priest and his body, (2) social solitude : the priest and his parishioners, (3) sacred solitude: the priest and the world of sin' – Schrader 1972: 72), somatising itself not only through the priest's disease-wracked biological body but also through the diary, the body of his writing that is also the writing of his body. He attempts to rediscover that God whose very absence, in a classic move of negative theology, is the clearest indication of His existence, via the ultimate gesture of submission-through-bodily-writing that is self-prostration in the form of the Cross. What the film actually shows is not that prostration, but his dejected rising to his feet afterwards, emphasising at this point result (or lack of it) rather than process. The apotheosis of the Cross is to take place not through the prison of the priest's body, but after he has left it.

Doctor Delbende, whom the priest has consulted over the pains in his stomach, commits suicide (the gunshot is heard off-screen). The priest's anguish over this is countered by the *curé* of Torcy's assertion: 'Le docteur Delbende était un homme juste. Dieu juge les justes'.[11] Judging – weighing in the balance, objectively, like against like – is precisely what the priest, given as he is to empathy and the taking on of responsibility, seems incapable of. Nor does the film invite us to judge as between the *curé* of Torcy's bluffness and the country priest's pain. To do so, indeed, would run counter to the complementarity of Church Militant and Church Suffering which the two priests incarnate.

Chantal visits the priest, denouncing her governess's affair with her father and manifesting intense hatred of her surroundings and, we may infer, of herself. The priest suspects that she may be contemplating suicide and asks her to give him the note she has written, which she does with an awestruck: 'Vous êtes donc le diable?'.[12] He throws it on the fire unread. This is the first of a series of spiritual confrontations and encounters that are to

---

11 'Doctor Delbende was a just man. God judges the just.' (NB: *not* 'a good man' as in the generally accurate but here misleading subtitles).
12 'Are you the devil?'

form the heart of the film, none more so than the priest's visit to
the countess shortly afterwards. The countess has withdrawn into
herself after the death of her adored young son some years before;
she clings to a medallion containing his photograph. In an
extraordinary scene accompanied by the sound of the gardener
raking leaves, the priest, perceiving that the countess's hatred of
God is still a relationship with Him, asks her to resign herself and
open her heart – a 'raking' of the long-dead embers of her spirit.
This is less a process of domination than it may appear, for the
priest is unable to look the countess in the eye when admitting his
fear of death to her, and his vulnerability is figured also by
Chantal's unseen presence outside the window. Repeating the
Lord's Prayer and accepting the priest's assurance that 'il n'y a pas
un royaume des vivants et un royaume des morts, il n'y a que le
royaume de Dieu, vivants ou morts, et nous sommes dedans'[13]
(Bernanos 1974: 191), she throws the medallion onto the fire from
which the priest retrieves it (live coals were used in the shooting).
She dies very soon after their meeting, not merely at peace with
herself but happy, though the priest's supposed meddling is
blamed for this and leads to his exclusion from the château. On
his last visit there, the priest – shot as if from the perspective of the
countess's dead body lying in the middle of the room – reflects
how strange it is that 'on puisse ainsi faire présent de ce qu'on ne
possède pas soi-même, ô doux miracle de nos mains vides!'[14]
(Bernanos 1974: 200). Jacques Derrida has written of 'la grande
mais discrète tradition de ce "donner ce qu'on n'a pas"'[15] (Derrida
1994: 204), which for him runs all the way from Plotinus to
Lacan. This film of the deepest spiritual loneliness and abjection
is at the same time, through such a paradoxical bestowing, an
enactment of the communion of saints, itself the supreme
expression of the transferability of merit with which the tradition
Derrida evokes is intimately linked.

13 'there is not a kingdom of the living and a kingdom of the dead, there is only
   God's kingdom and living or dead we are within it.'
14 'so we can make a gift of what we do not possess ourselves – oh, sweet miracle of
   our empty hands!'
15 'the great but discreet tradition of "giving what we do not have".'

The governess leaves, and the priest's physical and emotional state declines. Crossings-out become increasingly common in his diary. A conversation with the *curé* of Torcy makes it plain to him that his predestined place is on the Mount of Olives – the moment of uttermost solitude for Christ, abandoned by his disciples. He collapses on his rounds and is found by Séraphita Dumouchel, in a scene that along with the dialogue with the countess constitutes the spiritual heart of the film. The priest is seen leaning against a tree in a pose that explicitly recalls the Crucifixion, and in particular the two-dimensional Byzantine representations of Christ that Paul Schrader sees as major intertexts for Bresson (Schrader 1972: 100–1). It is shortly after this that, close to delirium, he has a vision of the face before which all must kneel – 'un visage d'enfant, [ou de très jeune fille,] sans aucun éclat'[16] (Bernanos 1974: 235). Jean Sémolué interprets this as a miraculous vision of the Virgin thanks to which the priest is able to dissuade Chantal from further self-destruction (Sémolué 1959: 174). This reading is likely to prove at least difficult for unorthodox or non-believing viewers, and furthermore seems to me to flatten out a diegetic ambiguity fundamental to the film. As the voiceover recounts the vision, the screen goes dark, to be followed by a close-up of Séraphita wiping the priest's face. 'In the novel, the face of God precedes the encounter with Séraphita; in the film, it seems to me that we are invited to identify the two, that the "face before which all must kneel" is quite literally Séraphita's' (Reader, 1990: 144). The question whether the vision is of God or the Virgin becomes on this reading peripheral, and indeed it may be superfluous to speak of a 'vision' *stricto sensu*. The priest's sight of Séraphita, the erstwhile tormentor become his saviour, is a sight of the face – divine, human, or both – before which all must kneel. 'Il n'y a que le royaume de Dieu, vivants ou morts, et nous sommes dedans'; yet for non-believers too the humanising of Bernanos's priest's vision makes it more accessible, one in a succession of 'conversions' in which previously hostile or indifferent women – Chantal, the countess, Séraphita – recognise

16 'The face of a child, [or a very young girl,] quite without splendour.' (The phrase in brackets is present in the novel but not pronounced in the film).

his spiritual power even in and through his moments of greatest weakness.

The priest has lost much blood and decides to go to Lille to consult a specialist. He is given a lift to the station by Chantal's cousin on his motorcycle – the one moment accorded to him in the film, perhaps in his life, of sheer physical exhilaration. The doctor diagnoses cancer of the stomach. He visits Dufréty, an old friend from seminary days, now working as a commercial traveller and living with the former nurse who had helped his recovery from a serious illness but has not wanted to marry him in case he should ever wish to return to the priesthood. This (unnamed) woman is the clearest example yet of a *femme douce* in Bresson's work, ministering to the terminally ill priest where Dufréty fatigues him with platitudes about his 'intellectual evolution'. The transparency of language for which the priest obviously yearns in vain through his diary is given to us here in the refreshing tenderness of the young woman's speech ('"Vous n'avez pas bonne mine non plus, monsieur, faut être juste!"'[17] (Bernanos 1974: 304)). *Écriture féminine*, a term associated with writers such as Marguerite Duras and Julia Kristeva which 'privileges the fluid, the convoluted and the mellifluous over the rational, the ordered, the univocal' (Hughes and Reader 1998: 173), does not seem an expression that might spring readily to mind in thinking about *Journal*; yet when Dufréty's companion says of suffering humanity, admittedly in a passage from the novel not included in the film, 'ça me fait comme un grand murmure qui me berce'[18] (Bernanos 1974: 304), it does have echoes of the feminised uses of language in its relationship with the body that were to become widespread from the 1970s onwards. Her voice, her language, cradle the dying priest at his moment of greatest need.

The final diary-writing sequence shows us the priest's exhausted hand moving across the page, but without the voice-over, as though in anticipation of his death – a sense which becomes more marked still when he drops his pen. The final sequence is pronounced by the *curé* of Torcy's voice as he reads a

17 'You don't look too good either, to tell the truth!'
18 'It's like a great whispering that rocks me.'

letter from Dufréty telling how the priest died. He asked his former colleague to absolve him, which Dufréty had reservations about doing since he was not in a state of grace. The priest 'a prononcé alors distinctement, bien qu'avec une extrême lenteur, ces mots que je suis sûr de rapporter très exactement: "Qu'est-ce que cela fait? Tout est grâce"'[19] (Bernanos 1974: 313), immediately before dying. The reading of the dying words is accompanied by the image of the Cross, which then fills the screen in silence.

The relationship between letter and spirit here is more complex than might at first appear. Bresson's film demonstrates remarkable, and appropriate, fidelity to the Bernanos text, as Dufréty does to his dying friend's words; yet excessive loyalty to the word is also possible, as Dufréty's dogmatic cavilling when the priest is at death's door illustrates. 'Tout est grâce' is at one and the same time an impeccably orthodox utterance, at any rate for God's elect in a Jansenist perspective, and a profoundly subversive one, disrespectful as it is of Church teachings on the state of grace. '"The letter kills, but the spirit gives life"; perhaps it is precisely Bresson's fetishistic literalness that, killing the letter with an excess of devotion, frees the spirit that would otherwise remain imprisoned' (Reader 1998: 429). For the final shot of the Cross, funereal as an account of it may appear, undoubtedly possesses a life-giving quality, not least because there is no body on it. The priest has left his suffering corporeal prison behind much as Mouchette is to do in Bresson's other Bernanos adaptation fifteen years later. The materiality of the bare Cross is all the more striking as a result. For Stefan Schädler, 'this Cross is only a sign, there is nothing beyond or "behind" it ... It is the prolongation, the summation of the film ... Bresson is materialist in his stress on suffering' (Buchka *et al.* 1978 [my translation]: 110). That materialism is the counterpart of the materialist stress on writing that has pervaded a film in which the suffering body and the body of writing meet as in scarcely any other. This is the sense in which we should understand Bazin's statement that 'la véritable structure selon

---

19 '[he] then pronounced distinctly, though extremely slowly, these words, which I am sure I am reporting quite exactly: "What does that matter? Everything is grace "'

laquelle se déroule le film est non pas celle de la tragédie mais celle du 'Jeu de la Passion' ou, mieux encore, celle du Chemin de Croix'[20] (Bazin 1985: 116). The faintings, the wiping of the priest's brow, his overpowering identification with the Mount of Olives make the analogy plain and help us to understand why on viewing the film – as usual with Bresson he had no access to the rushes – Laydu for the first time realised that he had been playing a saint.

The disappearance of images from the screen at the end, likened by Bazin to the 'dark night of the senses' of St John of the Cross, is the film's final exhaustion and transcendence of the possibilities of its language. 'Au point où en est arrivé Bresson l'image ne peut en dire davantage qu'en disparaissant'[21] (Bazin, 1985: 123). Exactly the same remark might be made about the written verbal language of the priest's diary. That too is 'only a sign, there is nothing beyond or "behind" it'; it is the process of writing his diary, not any definitive result it may bring, that has been important for the priest and the film. Simone Weil's maxim: 'Pour tout acte, le considérer sous l'aspect non de l'objet, mais de l'impulsion. Non pas: à quelle fin? Mais: d'où cela vient-il?'[22] (Weil 1988: 56) stresses the importance of process in a manner clearly applicable to Bresson's film. This is one reason why the voice-over, at once part of the process of writing and a commentary on it, is spiritually as well as materially fundamental to *Journal*. Writing and speech in this film, rather than being hierarchised, stand as undecidable recto and verso to each other, and it is the passage through and finally beyond them that leads to the transcendence of the final image. The body absent from the Cross is perhaps, *inter alia*, that of writing, as Bernard Chardère suggests when he compares the grey Cross at the end of *Journal* to Mallarmé's 'page blanche' (white or blank page) whose anguish precedes and haunts the writing process (Chardère 1952: 52).

Bazin's description of *Journal* as 'une phénoménologie du

---

20 'the real structure of the film is not that of tragedy but that of the "Passion Play" or, better still, of the Way of the Cross.'

21 'At the point Bresson has reached, the image can say more only by vanishing.'

22 'Consider any act from the point of view not of its object, but of what impels it. Not: to what end? But: where does this come from?'

salut et de la grâce'[23] (Bazin 1985: 118) likewise stresses the importance of process in the film – a process that has much in common with those of psychoanalysis. For Lacan, following Freud, 'the "talking cure" of analysis engages with language not as a seamless garment for ideas and meaning, but as a mechanism that produces sense(s) through its errors, hesitations, and silences' (Reader 1998: 428–9). To regard the diary as in some sense a 'writing cure' is certainly one way for the non-believer to read the film, and such a psychoanalytically based reading is given added credence by the scene between the priest and the countess. She is able to transcend her bitterness at least in part as the result of a transference onto the priest of the maternal feelings she has jealously guarded for her dead son; her letter to him makes this plain in saying 'il me semble qu'un autre enfant m'a tirée de cette solitude'[24] (Bernanos 1974: 195). In her confrontation with the priest as in the psychoanalytic process, 'les paroles prononcées ne sont pourtant que les temps morts, l'écho du silence qui est le vrai dialogue de ces deux âmes, une allusion à leur secret: le côté pile, – si l'on ose dire, – de la Face de Dieu'[25] (Bazin 1985: 120). That 'côté pile', and what it implies about speech, writing and silence, is of supreme importance in *Journal*, it seems to me, even for those for whom 'la Face de Dieu' is not a meaningful concept.

References

Andrew, Dudley (1984), *Film in the Aura of Art*, Princeton and Guildford, Princeton University Press.

Bazin, André (1985), *Qu'est-ce que le cinéma?* Paris, Cerf.

Bernanos, Georges (1974), *Journal d'un curé de campagne*, Paris, Plon.

Briot, René (1957), *Robert Bresson*, Paris, Cerf.

Buchka, Peter, Prinzler, Hans Helmut, Schädler, Stefan and Vitte, Karsten (1978), *Robert Bresson*, Munich, Hansen.

23 'a phenomenology of salvation and grace.'

24 'It seems to me that another child has taken me out of that solitude.'

25 'the words spoken are merely lulls, the echo of the silence that is the real dialogue of these two souls, an allusion to their secret: the obverse, if I dare say so, of the Face of God.'

Burch, Noël and Sellier, Geneviève (1996), *Le 'drôle de guerre' des sexes du cinéma français*, Paris, Nathan.

Chardère, Bernard (1952), article in *Positif*, 3: 51–6.

Deleuze, Gilles (1985), *Cinéma 2: L'Image-temps*, Paris, Minuit.

Derrida, Jacques (1994), *Politiques de l'amitié*, Paris, Galilée.

Droguet, Robert (1966), *Robert Bresson*, Premier Plan 42, Lyon.

Hughes, Alex and Reader, Keith (eds) (1998), *Encyclopedia of Contemporary French Culture*, London and New York, Routledge.

Mauriac, François (1997), 'Journal d'un curé de campagne,' in *Robert Bresson: Éloge*, Milan and Paris, Mazzotta/Cinémathèque française.

Reader, Keith (1990), 'The sacrament of writing: Robert Bresson's *Le Journal d'un curé de campagne* (1951), in Susan Hayward and Ginette Vincendeau (eds), *French Film: Texts and contexts*, London and New York, Routledge.

Reader, Keith (1998), '"D'où cela vient-il?": notes on three films by Robert Bresson', in James Quandt (ed.), *Robert Bresson*, Cinémathèque Ontario, Toronto.

Ropars-Wuillemier, Marie-Claire (1970), *De la littérature au cinéma: genèse d'une écriture*, Paris, Armand Colin.

Schrader, Paul (1972), *Transcendental Style in Film: Ozu, Bresson, Dreyer*, Los Angeles and London, University of California Press.

Sémolué, Jean (1959), *Robert Bresson*, Paris, Éditions Universitaires.

Weil, Simone (1988), *La Pesanteur et la grâce*, Paris, Plon.

3

The 'prison cycle': *Un Condamné à mort s'est échappé, Pickpocket* and *Le Procès de Jeanne d'Arc*

Un Condamné à mort s'est échappé

Un Condamné à mort s'est échappé, released in 1956, was and remains Bresson's most commercially successful and critically best-received film, though curiously for a very long time it was unavailable in Britain (it was for many years the only Bresson feature I had never seen). Its Resistance setting and subject-matter were largely responsible for this, though as Sylvie Lindeperg points out the film 'relègue la dimension temporelle de l'événement dans un hors-champ sonore, et la Résistance, dépouillée de son historicité, s'y trouve réduite au rang d'expérience mentale'[1] (Lindeperg 1996: 261). The film is based on André Devigny's account of his real-life escape from the Montluc prison in Lyon – the very prison in which Klaus Barbie had had Jean Moulin tortured to death and in which he was himself subsequently to be incarcerated. Yet *Un Condamné* is anything but a 'Resistance film', in the sense in which that term can be applied to Melville's *L'Armée des ombres* or more recently Berri's *Lucie Aubrac*. All we know of the activities which have led Fontaine, the protagonist, to be arrested and condemned to death is that he is alleged to have blown up a railway bridge – an archetypal Resistance activity, as in Clément's *La Bataille du rail*. Nor is there ever any allusion to the rightness and urgency of the

---

[1] 'relegates the time dimension of the event to off-screen sound, so that the Resistance, deprived of its historical quality, is reduced to a mental experience.'

cause. The word 'Resistance', indeed, is not pronounced, so that Adelio Ferrero's description of the film as 'the most poetic and intransigent affirmation of [the] Resistance ... in its most irreducible and extreme form' (Ferrero 1976: 47 (my translation)) seems to me justified only if the term is all but voided of any historical content, evoking instead an individual process and state of mind, or even soul, whose intense spirituality is complemented and vehicled by its equally intense materiality.

That materiality is heightened by, on the one hand, the film's claustrophobic setting, and, on the other, its tightly focused use of sound, well analysed by Michel Chion. *Un Condamné* seems to me the first Bresson film to which his injunction 'Lorsqu'un son peut remplacer une image, supprimer l'image ou la neutraliser'[2] is fully applicable, for crucial though the sound clearly is in *Journal* it still functions there as complement or equal partner to the image. The repeated sequences in *Un Condamné* in which the prisoners empty their slop-buckets to the sound of Mozart's Mass in C minor, on the other hand, owe their force to an interplay of the degrading and the sublime accessible only via the soundtrack. The claustrophobia of the setting focuses our attention upon the sound, most strikingly in the scenes in which Fontaine is working towards his escape with the aid of a spoon and metal instruments fashioned from the furnishings of his cell. The sounds here are literally the matter of life and death.

The fact that *Un Condamné* is set in a prison might be thought to make it as it were *ex officio* claustrophobic. René Prédal speaks of prison in Bresson's work (not just the three films, of which *Un Condamné* is the first, set in whole or in part in prison) as 'à la fois métaphore de l'existence et condition nécessaire à tout exercice du cinématographe'.[3] We have seen how the priest's body in *Journal* acts as a prison in the first of Prédal's senses. In *Un Condamné*, the second sense becomes plainer. François Leterrier's question suggests how the escape of Fontaine – the character he plays – might be read as a *mise en abyme* of the film's making, and the

2 See above.
3 At once a metaphor for existence and a necessary condition for any cinematographic exercise.'

prison itself as the world of cinema as opposed to cinematography ('Pourquoi ce film énigmatique ne serait-il pas son propre journal de tournage? Fontaine, Bresson en train de créer Fontaine? Et l'évasion, l'image fidèle de cette entreprise patiemment menée à bien?')[4] (Leterrier 1956: 35).

Films about prison and escape – from Grémillon's *La Petite Lise* through to Becker's *Le Trou* – have been a fairly regular feature of French as of Hollywood cinema, but it would be as much of a category mistake to place *Un Condamné* in this genre as to regard it as a 'Resistance film'. Truffaut, himself no stranger to the penitential system, recognised as much when he compared it to a film which devotes equivalent attention to the mechanisms of 'escape' although these are being used to break in – to a jeweller's vault – rather than out. 'J'avais écrit, par exemple, un article très favorable sur *Du Rififi chez les hommes*, de Jules Dassin; et puis, en voyant *Un Condamné à mort s'est échappé*, je me suis dit: "Ça, c'est tout de même autre chose"' (Truffaut and Lantil-Le Dantec 1997: 87).[5] One intertext often evoked by Bresson's film, of which it is in many ways the antithesis, is Renoir's *La Grande Illusion*, set in the less menacing, indeed sometimes uneasily jovial, atmosphere of an officers' prison camp during the First World War. Truffaut implicitly recognised this in his eulogy of the Bresson film in *Arts*, in which he says of Fontaine 'ce n'est pas le courage qui l'incite à s'évader, mais l'ennui, l'oisiveté; une prison est faite pour s'en évader'[6] (Truffaut 1975: 217). The last phrase is a direct quotation from Pierre Fresnay/Captain de Boeldieu in *La Grande Illusion*. The Renoir film has an openness and a socio-historical acuteness entirely absent from *Un Condamné*, yet the barked orders from the German guards, the uneasy fraternity between the prisoners, the two escapees precariously together at the end are features

4 'Why might this enigmatic film not be the record of its own shooting? Fontaine, Bresson in the process of creating Fontaine? And the escape the faithful image of this patiently carried through undertaking?'
5 'I had written, for example, a very favourable piece on *Du Rififi chez les hommes*, by Jules Dassin; and then I saw *Un Condamné à mort s'est échappé*, and said to myself: "That is really something else".'
6 'it is not courage that incites him to escape, but boredom and idleness; a prison is made to be escaped from.'

common to both. So too is the importance of chance factors, notably a change of prison at the crucial time. For Renoir, this is one indication among many of how History with a capital H is ultimately dependent on the aleatory ramifications of a host of little *histoires*/histories; in that sense, *La Grande Illusion* is a supremely secular film. For Bresson, on the other hand, it implies the presence of grace, never more inescapably at work, as the whole of *Journal* suggests, than in the way in which we write the narratives of our lives. 'Il a fallu qu'Orsini rate pour que tu réussisses':[7] Blanchet's observation to Fontaine, like the ending of *Journal*, demonstrates how the tragic that inhabits the seemingly trivial can be in the most literal sense redeemed, bought back, through the retroactive narrativising logic of grace.

The very title, a bald factual assertion, immediately undercuts the suspense normally deemed essential to an escape film, and the shot of Montluc prison, with its accompanying voice-over assuring us that what we are about to see really happened, lends the opening a quasi-documentary tone. The role of the voice-over in *Un Condamné* is more straightforward, because less recursive, than in *Journal*, attesting to the 'truth' of the events on screen and sometimes providing information that the necessarily whispered and furtive conversations within the prison cannot. It also situates the film's documentary quality firmly in the first person, a 'point de vue documenté' as Jean Vigo had described his *A propos de Nice* (Salles Gomes 1957: 83). Bazin points out that for all its concentration on the minutiae of physical detail the film demonstrates an 'indifférence systématique au temps et à l'espace'[8] manifest in its refusal of any overall topographic perspective; to draw a plan of the prison, on the basis of the information the film gives us, would be an impossibility. This absence of 'géométrie dramatique'[9] (Bazin 1997: 31), along with the film's narrative structure, makes *Un Condamné* the very reverse of a 'suspense film' in the conventional sense of the term.

Bresson's *modèles* here, as ever, were on the whole drawn from

7 'Orsini had to fail for you to succeed.'
8 'systematic indifference to time and space.'
9 'dramatic geometry.'

the comfortable bourgeois milieu of his acquaintance – François Leterrier a philosophy teacher, Roland Monod, who plays the Protestant pastor Deleyris, a drama critic and journalist. Louis Malle commented, in his introduction to the British television screening of the film, on the uncanny likeness between Charles le Clainche/François Jost and Pierre Blaise, who played the collaborationist title character in Malle's 1973 film *Lacombe Lucien*. Malle even suggests that he was unconsciously influenced by the Bresson film in his casting of Blaise. Fontaine's doubts about Jost's reliability – concretised by his turning up in the cell wearing a mixture of French and German uniforms – certainly suggest a possible resemblance between the two characters that goes beyond the merely physiognomic.

After the view of Montluc, we see Fontaine in a Gestapo car between two officers. He forces open the door and makes a run for it, but is brought back, handcuffed and beaten. The stress here, as so often throughout the film, is on hands and their actions – picking handcuffs, forcing locks, shaping the instruments of escape – in accordance with the 'phénoménologie du salut et de la grâce' Bazin evokes in his reading of *Journal*.[10] *Un Condamné* is the only Bresson film – unless we count Joan of Arc as the first Protestant – to include a Protestant character, the aforementioned pastor who in prison ironically fulfils his dream of being alone with his Bible. This quietism and Fontaine's devouring need to escape can be seen as representing respectively the Protestant justification by faith and the Catholic justification by works. Later, when the pastor advises 'Lisez et priez, Dieu vous sauvera', Fontaine replies: 'Ce serait trop commode si Dieu se chargeait de tout'.[11] Grace in its paradoxical action demands human striving for divine providence to make itself felt – a striving manual and spiritual at once, epitomised in that Catholic tradition that encompasses the old monastic adage 'laborare est orare' ('to work is to pray') and George Herbert's 'Who sweeps a room as for Thy laws/ Makes that and th'action fine' (Herbert [*c*. 1635] 1994: 171).

10 See above, pp. 40–1.
11 'Read and pray, God will save you ... It would be too easy if God took care of everything.'

Fontaine's initial dash for freedom, futile on one level as it is, is the first manifestation of that necessary striving.

We see Fontaine in his cell, face covered in blood. The first contact he makes is with Terry, walking with two others in the courtyard, who passes up to him some paper and a pencil. The constraints of the surroundings account for the fleeting and often enigmatic quality of the conversations, here and elsewhere, so that on a first viewing we may not even think to ask where Deleyris's Bible mysteriously appears from or how Terry has been able to get the pencil and paper for Fontaine. His neighbour in the next cell, whom he never sees but with whom he communicates by tapping out messages on the wall, tells him how to open his handcuffs with a pin, which he manages to do. Moved to another cell, he is able to open a gap in the wood of the door with a spoon. Chion's analysis distinguishes five sonic spaces – within the cell (necessarily circumscribed since Fontaine's activity is clandestine); in the prison around the cell, more reverberant and hinting at a space greater than what the camera shows us; in the city outside the prison (passing trams and cars, children's cries); outside the city (the periodic train-whistles, which evoke both the reason for Fontaine's imprisonment and his need to escape); and finally, the non-diegetic sound – what Chion describes as sound 'off' – of the Mozart music in the slopping-out sequences, jubilantly reprised at the end (Chion 1992: 38–39). The scraping noise – methodical, even tiresomely so – of Fontaine's spoon is thus at one extreme of a kind of ladder or chain of sound which culminates in the Mozart, the sublime inhabiting the humble which is its necessary precondition.

One day as the prisoners line up to empty their buckets, Fontaine helps Blanchet, his elderly neighbour, hitherto unresponsive to his attempts at communication. Blanchet sees no point in struggling to escape, having no family or friends. Fontaine exhorts him 'Luttez pour tous ceux qui sont ici'[12] – an echo of the cause that has presumably brought them all there, but also of the communion of saints of which the prison is a microcosm. Orsini,

---

12 'Struggle for all those who are here.'

the prisoner whose cell is opposite Fontaine's and who becomes his accomplice, has been betrayed by his wife, yet is described as beyond hatred and suffering. For him, 'c'est comme si c'était arrivé à un autre'.[13] Orsini's transformation is nowhere 'explained'; psychological explanation, we have seen, is foreign to Bresson's universe, never more so than to these prisoners shut off from their 'real lives' outside. If *Un Condamné* has attracted less hostile criticism than Bresson's other films, it is at least in part because the setting acts to justify a 'totale indifférence ... aux problèmes de vraisemblance'[14] (Bazin 1997: 30) present throughout his work, and the target of some of its severest attacks.

Orsini's transformation is soon to be mirrored by that of Blanchet, who after Orsini has been caught trying to escape and shot encourages Fontaine with the already-quoted words: 'Il a fallu qu'Orsini rate pour que tu réussisses'. Fontaine's response to this – 'L'extraordinaire, c'est que c'est vous, M. Blanchet, qui le dites'[15] – constructs Blanchet as Paraclete and annunciator, spiritual comforter and bearer of transcendental tidings. Once again, the bizarre conditions and systemic role-reversals of the prison environment make this exchange readily accessible to a non-transcendental reading. *Un Condamné* can be viewed as a 'spiritual realist' film in the sense in which the films of Carné and Prévert are often described as 'poetic realist', with the crucial difference that the Bresson film operates metonymically rather than, like Carné's, metaphorically. The one-eyed teddy-bear in *Le Jour se lève* is a fairly clear metaphor for Jean Gabin/François's gruff vulnerability. Fontaine's spoon, the metal support of his bed, his enigmatic exchanges with Blanchet and others derive their force not from any such poetics of character, but from their juxtaposition with one another, adventitious and inevitable at once.

Thus it is that, if Orsini's failure has been necessary for Fontaine to succeed, it has also catalysed a radical change in Blanchet. The passage from St John's Gospel to which the pastor

13 'it's as if it had happened to somebody else.'
14 'a total indifference ... to questions of plausibility'.
15 'The extraordinary thing is that you, M. Blanchet, are telling me that.'

directs Fontaine's attention, and which says that 'the wind bloweth where it listeth', also speaks of the need to be born again. So overgrown with evangelical cliché has that phrase now become that it may seem to have lost all credibility, yet the abrupt external severances and internal changes that many characters in this film undergo make it peculiarly appropriate here. Orsini's 'rebirth' has taken place before our first encounter with him; Blanchet's is attested by his remark to Fontaine; we are to witness Jost's in the final sequences; and Fontaine's is in a sense the true subject-matter – the ultimate 'narrated' – of the film. An indication of what such an experience might be like in a non-Christian context is given by Sartre's Mathieu Delarue in *La Mort dans l'âme*, who after shooting a German soldier reflects: 'ce coup-ci, on ne lui avait rien volé du tout. Il avait appuyé sur la gâchette et, pour une fois, quelque chose était arrivé. "Quelque chose de définitif", pensa-t-il en riant de plus belle'[16] (Sartre 1949: 271). The different context – one of personal frustration transcending itself to issue in political commitment – throws into relief the similarities between Delarue's defining experience of change and that of Fontaine.

The prisoners are told to hand over any pencils on pain of death; Fontaine denies possession of one, immediately after which his voice-over tells us: 'Quelle bêtise!'.[17] That 'bêtise', of course, is a sign at once of his attachment to the vestiges of his linguistic humanity and of his increasing inability to comply with the laws of captivity. The parcel of clothes sent to him – by whom we never know – is ruthlessly shredded to be converted into ropes. He confides in Blanchet that the hardest thing is to decide, a performative act of speech if ever there were – to say it is already at least in part to have decided. Once he has been taken to the Hôtel Terminus and been told that he is to be shot, the decision is made for him, and Jost's arrival in his cell poses only the problem of whether he should kill him or enlist him in his escape. Jost is a disturbing presence in more ways than one, for to his ambiguous

16 'this time, nothing at all had been stolen from him. He had squeezed the trigger and, for once, something had happened. "Something definitive", he thought, laughing even louder.'
17 'How stupid!'

uniform, half French, half German, corresponds an androgynous quality marked when he speaks of the beauty of his mother and sister, and particularly troubling in this film which has just one female presence on screen – a prisoner glimpsed very briefly in the background near the beginning. Fontaine's insistence in clinging on to his pencil may have appeared bizarre, since he has not subsequently needed to use it. Yet it acquires what might quite properly be called a sacramental value when he shares the secret of its possession, and the risk he is running, with the incredulous Jost. Infinite value, we have seen, can inhere in the most modest of objects or activities, in a manner that may put us in mind of René Briot's reminder that images for Bresson have above all exchange value. The secret of the pencil forges a bond between Fontaine and Jost which makes any turning back or retreat impossible. The final section of the film is as tense and exhilarating by turns as almost anything in the conventional cinema of suspense, compressing a four-and-a-half-hour escape into some ten minutes. Fontaine kills a German soldier – off-screen, as in a Racine tragedy – and as Jost helps him to climb another wall reflects in voice-over: 'Seul, je serais peut-être resté là'.[18] They cross the final gap monkey-fashion, arms and legs clinging to the stretched rope, and jump to the ground, where Fontaine cradles his accomplice and pronounces his name: 'Jost'. Jost's response ('Si ma mère me voyait!')[19] dispels the tension of the previous moments with a mixture of innocent pride, disbelief and the strong albeit unstated sense that he has just undergone a rite of passage into manhood. Bresson has often enough been accused of lacking a sense of humour, yet there are moments in his work to which a fit response seems to be a seriously amused smile, none more so for me than Jost's final exclamation. A train covers the two escapees in its smoke as nineteen years before Jean Gabin/Maréchal and Marcel Dalio/Rosenthal had disappeared into dots on the snow in *La Grande Illusion*, and we hear Mozart once more – this time acting as consecration not only of the escape, but of the catharsis so splendidly effected by Jost's words.

18 'On my own, I might have remained there.'
19 'If my mother could see me!'

The trivial and the sublime remain joyously together at the end of *Un Condamné* as they have done throughout the film.

Pickpocket

Pickpocket is widely recognised as marking a key break in Bresson's work. The first of his films not to be based on a text written by somebody else, it is perceived by Michel Estève as marking his final break with the classic French cinema of earlier years and sharing with New Wave film-makers such as Rohmer and Godard 'une conception moderne du cinéma'[20] (Estève 1983: 10). Philippe Arnaud contrasts it to *Un condamné* – with which it has much in common, notably the prison theme and the use of music – by observing: 'Autant le *Condamné* était le film d'une volonté inflexible, et consciente, autant *Pickpocket* annexe, pour le cinéma, le domaine neuf des automatismes inconscients: la main, sa volonté quasi-autonome, en est le guide'[21] (Arnaud 1986: 28). The 'automatismes inconscients' in question are clearly connected with Bresson's idea of the *modèle*, refined in this film to a higher degree than before. In the light of Michel's, and the film's, final words – 'O Jeanne, pour aller jusqu'à toi, quel drôle de chemin il m'a fallu prendre!'[22] – it would be possible to speak of *Pickpocket* as 'le film d'une volonté inflexible, et inconsciente'. Michel's seeming perversity, manifested in his reluctance to visit his mother until the very last, his rebuffs of Jacques's and Jeanne's attempts to help him, his self-destructive persistence in thieving, is revealed *ex post facto* as the agent of his redemption. The criticism sometimes levelled against the director that, like Mauriac for Sartre in *Qu'est-ce que la littérature?*, he imposes salvation upon his characters, is justified of this film perhaps more than of any other Bresson film. Yet it seems to me largely countered by,

20 'a modern conception of cinema.'
21 'Just as *Un Condamné* was the film of a consciously inflexible will, so *Pickpocket* annexes for the cinema the new realm of unconscious automatic gesture, guided by the hand and its quasi-autonomous will.'
22 'Oh Jeanne, to reach you, what a strange path I had to take!'

precisely, the 'automatismes inconscients' of Michel's countenance and gestures – a series of parapraxes that at once invite and
call into question a Freudian reading of his actions, constructing
him all the time as 'a submitting object of processes that
transcend him'[23] and situating those processes within as much as
beyond him.

The film was shot in the summer of 1959, more or less at the
same time as Godard's *A bout de souffle*, and begins with a genre
disclaimer ('Ce film n'est pas du style policier')[24] that a few
moments' viewing will be enough to corroborate. Features of
Bresson's other work, notably the often simultaneous use of voice-
over and a written record, are apparent, but refined by an ascesis
to which the film's unusually short running-time of seventy-five
minutes and the flattened-out filming of Martin Lasalle/Michel's
haunted features bear witness. Bresson speaks of the voice-over
commentary as 'un élément de plus qui *agit* sur les autres
éléments du film, qui les *modifie*'[25] (Arnaud 1986: 179) – truer for
Pickpocket even than for *Journal* because the later film's commentary is clearly written after rather than during the narrated action.
Its opening phrases, written by Michel in his cell – 'D'habitude
ceux qui font ces choses ne les écrivent pas, et pourtant je les ai
faites'[26] – invite us to read the film as confessional autobiography
and Michel's retroactive commentary as metatext articulating its/
his most essential truth. Yet the absence of psychological detail, the
lack of evident causal or temporal relations between the sequences,
the pared-down matter of factness of the commentary undercut
such readings, or rather shift their centre of gravity away from the
explicable and totalisable towards what Freud in another context
called *ein anderer Schauplatz* ('the scene of action ... is different'
(Freud [1900] 1976: 112)). That other context is, precisely, *The
Interpretation of Dreams*, and the dreamlike quality of much of
Pickpocket, at once hyperreal and redolent of the Freudian

23 See p. 5.
24 'This is not a film in the detective style.'
25 'an extra element which *acts* upon the other elements of the film, *modifying*
   them.'
26 'Usually those who do these things do not write about them, and yet I did/have
   done them.'

Unheimliche/uncanny, suggests analogies between Michel's odyssey of transformation and the psychoanalytic process as well as the operations of grace. The film, shot on location in Paris, gives us no sense of neighbourhood (though the commentary tells us that Michel meets his accomplice in the Barbès-Rochechouart area, near Montmartre), nor of chronological time. Michel, like the country priest, keeps a diary, yet it would be impossible to say how long a period the action of either film spans; the only temporality *Pickpocket* recognises is Michel's lived, existential time. If, according to Louis Malle – a non-believer – 'pour le temps de la projection, l'artiste est Dieu'[27] (Malle 1997), this suggests less hubris than a demiurgic intensity of concentration that dismisses all not relevant to its purpose. 'The director behind the camera, like the analyst behind the couch, can readily be likened to God – superficially absent but everywhere implicit in the world (the film, the discourse) he creates' (Reader 1998: 439). Michel's journal and commentary in this light represent the film's 'truth' metonymically, as part of its workings, rather than standing in a metaphoric or transcendental relation to it. Thus it is that at the end the status of his final words, spoken but not transcribed in the journal, is ambiguous. As David Bordwell says, 'we cannot tell if it is a line of dialogue he murmurs to her, or the final voice-over commentary' (Bordwell 1985: 309). That undecidability, which calls into question the status of the journal and the commentary as metatext, is fundamental to the rhetoric of grace in *Pickpocket*, preventing us from situating Michel's salvation unequivocally either within or outside himself. Antoine Cervoni said as early as 1963 that 'Bresson nous donne un cinéma de l'événement et non de l'intériorité'[28] (*Cinéma 6*: 30) – the 'event' to be understood here, as subsequently in the work of Lyotard, as that which 'refuses to be absorbed into the *order* of a classical narrative, brought to book in a narrative *account*, its tension exchanged for other tensions' (Bennington 1988: 109). 'A narrative account' of the film and of the redemption it operates is precisely what I am about to attempt, but the constitutive impossibility of such a task should be kept in mind.

After the opening sequence, Michel is seen at the Longchamp racecourse, plucking up courage and finally stealing banknotes from a woman's handbag. There is an *unheimlich* quality to this sequence that derives in large part from the use of sound, for while we hear the ticket-machines clattering away like the mechanisms of destiny we do not hear the voices of the punters as they place their bets. We are to find this use of sound developed later in the film. Michel's exhilaration at his success ('Je n'avais plus les pieds sur terre. Je dominais le monde')[29] already suggests drives behind the theft other than those of everyday materialism – erotic, to be sure, but also transcendental, seeking the state of weightlessness suggested in Simone Weil's *La Pesanteur et la grâce* and, in connection with Bresson, by Susan Sontag ('The true fight against oneself is against one's heaviness, one's gravity' (Sontag 1964: 17)). Weightlessness, closely associated in the Christian mystical tradition with rising up towards God (see the paintings of El Greco), has already been figured by the disappearance of the priest's body at the end of *Journal*. Michel's ecstasy at the beginning of *Pickpocket*, however, is short-lived; he is arrested, but rapidly released for lack of proof. Back 'home' – in his sparsely furnished room, comically so perhaps by today's standards but not atypical of how many less well-off younger people lived in the Paris of the time – he reflects, exhausted, on the need to 'mettre de l'ordre dans mes idées'.[30] Bresson has often said that he regards himself as less a *metteur en scène* than a *metteur en ordre*. In his mother's block of flats, he runs into her young neighbour Jeanne to whom he gives money for her, yet he refuses to go in and see her – the first indication of the troubled relationship with her that may tempt a psycho-hermeneutic interpretation of the film. To quote Daniel Millar:

> Michel's relationship with his mother has been a favourite area for probing, since he refuses to see her until she is seriously ill – in

29 'My feet no longer touched the ground. I dominated the world.'
30 'to sort my ideas out.'

fact, dying – and then expresses affection for her. From here it is a
short Freudian step to the inspector as friendly yet rejected father-
figure, and then to the gestures of theft as surreptitious caresses,
so that Michel's final declaration of love for Jeanne becomes his
renunciation of his repressed homosexuality. (Millar 1962: 89)

Renunciation and repression apart, this will be familiar terrain
for readers of Genet, and it is difficult to deny the homoerotic
component in many of the pickpocketing scenes, or the Oedipal
dimension of Michel's stealing from his mother. Yet to reduce the
film to an allegorical voyage through or 'growing out of' homosexuality would be grossly reductive, undermining Bresson's
'cinéma de l'événement' in favour of the cinema of interiority it
emphatically is not. T. Jefferson Kline offers a subtler view of
Michel's pickpocketing through stressing its fetishistic element
and the workings of this at the level of the film's structure: 'The
real thing has been disavowed. The pleasure is always elsewhere:
in the hand, in the money, wallets, watches removed from the
victims – fragments. Just as in the making of the film the pleasure
itself is located in fragmentation, a pleasure of the fetishized eye'
(Kline 1992: 183). That '*real* thing', evidently connected with the
mother, may then be that which returns so powerfully with and
through Jeanne at the end of the film, though we shall see that
Kline has reservations about such a reading.

Michel goes on to a café to meet his somewhat superior friend
Jacques, who provides him with a list of addresses where he may
find work and even become the owner of a new suit or a tie – a
smugly materialist attitude which may provoke a derision in the
audience analogous to that expressed by Ewan MacGregor's Mark
in the opening sequence of Danny Boyle's *Trainspotting*. Also in
the café is the police inspector who earlier questioned Michel, and
who now hears him expound – self-incriminatingly? – his view
that there are superior human beings to whom normal codes of
morality do not apply. Nietzsche's Superman, Gide's Lafcadio in
Les Caves du Vatican, above all Dostoevsky's Raskolnikov in *Crime
and Punishment* articulate similar philosophies. Dostoevsky's
influence upon Bresson is a matter of record, marked in this film
most clearly by the empathy that develops between Michel and the

inspector as between Porfiry and Raskolnikov. Shot/reverse-shot is used more in this scene than elsewhere in the film, emphasising that Michel is perhaps for the first time in his life in a relationship of real reciprocity, to become conceivably as important as his love for Jeanne of which it is in many ways the condition and counterpart.

On the metro, Michel spots another pickpocket at work, and observes his technique. Jeanne is anxious about the declining health of Michel's mother, but he insists on being left alone. He meets another pickpocket – a role played by Kassagi, who had actually 'worked' as a pickpocket in North Africa and acted as technical advisor to the film, of which he was strongly to disapprove. Kassagi teaches him tricks of the trade, filmed in quasi-documentary close-up to music by Lulli. These scenes, and others to follow, are reminiscent of the pail-emptying episodes in *Un condamné*. Here, however, the grace figured by the music is at work in circumstances not imposed upon the central character, but chosen by him – a distinction at first sight perhaps more important than it may come to appear in the light of the complex dialectic of grace and free will that drives both films. Has Michel 'chosen' pickpocketing, or has it 'chosen' him? To such a question, Bresson's theological apparatus, like his cinematography, makes an unequivocal answer impossible.

Michel finds, the day after it has been delivered, a note from Jeanne begging him to go to his mother's bedside. His mother speaks warmly to him and tells him that she understands him – a reference to his thefts from her? He assures her that she will live; in an audacious juxtaposition that is to be characteristic of the Bresson of this period, there is an immediate cut to her funeral service, Michel shedding a tear for the first time in the film. Later he denounces to Jeanne the idea of divine judgement, and when she asks whether he believes in anything replies: 'J'ai cru en Dieu, Jeanne, pendant trois minutes'.[31] Michel's remark on the face of it confirms Jean-Claude Brisseau's view that *Pickpocket* inaugurates a stage in Bresson's career where 'c'est l'absence de Dieu qui

31 'I believed in God, Jeanne, for three minutes.'

règne'[32] (*Cahiers du cinéma*, 1989: 30). He has generally been thought to be referring to his mother's funeral, but the evidence for that is largely circumstantial and unconvincing – non-believers are quite as likely to weep on such occasions. It could equally well apply to the moment of weightlessness we have seen him experience when committing his first 'public' theft – a moment of hubris in which he 'dominated the world' like (a) God. It is clearly not material ambition that draws him back to thieving – he continues to live in a shabby room – so much as the *jouissance*, in the Barthesian sense, that the act procures for him. For Barthes, *jouissance* is 'hors de toute finalité imaginable – *même celle du plaisir* (la jouissance n'oblige pas au plaisir; elle peut même apparemment ennuyer). Aucun alibi ne tient, rien ne se reconstitue, rien ne se récupère. Le texte de jouissance est absolument intransitif'[33] (Barthes 1973: 83). This concept, more perhaps even than Kline's fragmented pleasure, is helpful in thinking the furtive – from the Latin for 'thief' – and homoerotic aspects of Michel's actions without collapsing them into the kind of naive Freudian allegory outlined by Millar.

A third pickpocket joins Michel and his companion, this one played by Pierre Étaix who worked with Jacques Tati before becoming a comic actor and director in his own right. Jacques, Jeanne and Michel go to a fair, though a less joyous, more imprisoning occasion it would be difficult to imagine; we see nothing of the rides and machines (they will have to wait until *Mouchette*), and Michel is obviously anxious to be off. Where to we discover only in ambiguous retrospect, seeing Michel washing off blood in his room and clutching a stolen watch. Far more festive than the fair is the following sequence, one of modern cinema's great bravura passages and compared by Sitney to the rabbit-hunt in Renoir's *La Règle du jeu* as the epicentre of the film (Sitney 1998: 158). Michel and his accomplices pick pockets and steal

32 'God's absence is dominant.'

33 'outside any imaginable finality – *even that of pleasure* (*jouissance* does not necessarily entail pleasure; it can even appear tedious). No alibi stands up, nothing can be reconstituted or recuperated. The *jouissance*-text is absolutely intransitive.'

watches in the Gare de Lyon. The autonomous will of the hand evoked by Arnaud[34] here reaches its apotheosis. For Gilles Deleuze the space of *Pickpocket* is above all a tactile one, bringing together 'espaces à fragmentation' similar to those we have seen in *Un condamné* into 'une adéquation de l'espace avec l'affect exprimé comme potentialité pure'[35] (Deleuze 1983: 154). Michel is in the most literal sense feeling his way towards redemption, and our inability to see as a whole the spaces – the racecourse, the fairground, the station concourse – in which he operates, corresponds to his inability to see the wider space, the *anderer Schauplatz*, in which his destiny is playing (or working) itself out. Noël Burch has drawn attention to the importance of empty and off-screen space for Bresson, notably in *Pickpocket* and *Un condamné* (Burch 1969: 43–4), but that space, here even more than in the earlier film, goes beyond the formal just as it does beyond the visual.

Michel, after a visit from the inspector, hastens to Jeanne and forces her to understand that he had stolen from his mother. He asks her to shake his hand and she holds him in her arms, thereby taking her undisputed place among the *femmes douces* in Bresson's work. Michel leaves, first for Milan, then for Rome and London, without so much as closing the door to his room, and returns after two years wearing the same suit. Bresson's anti-naturalism, always insistent in its materiality, here reaches a peak. On his return, he discovers Jeanne with a child she has borne to Jacques, whom she has refused to marry because she does not love him and who has broken all contact with her. The appearance of respectability has been a cover for pharisaic hypocrisy, not for the last time in Bresson. Michel takes a job and hands his pay over to Jeanne – the first and only incidence of anything so Protestant as a work ethic in Bresson – but is drawn back to Longchamp, where the clattering of the machines reminds us of the beginning and brings the film full circle. He picks a final pocket and is arrested; in prison, Jeanne visits him, but then cannot come for several weeks because her child is sick. Despair is averted when she comes again, and the two embrace silently through the bars (an

34 See p. 52.
35 'fragmented spaces ... an equation of space with pure affective potentiality.'

ending to be reprised by Paul Schrader in his first film as director, *American Gigolo*). The Lulli music is heard one last time as Michel's voice reflects on the 'drôle de chemin' he has had to take.

Kline mistrusts the intimations of grace in this final scene, which he sees as 'remarkably ambiguous' (Kline 1992: 167). Yet it was the first Bresson sequence to move the then Bresson-sceptical me to tears, and on repeated viewings its impact remains undiminished. Part of the reason is, I think, that however much he may disclaim influence from, or even knowledge of, other films the director here is clearly and deliberately playing with the conventional cinematic idea of the happy ending – a convention with which the Schrader film is much more obviously complicit. If the happy ending represents, in Kristevan terms, a restoration of the imaginary plenitude of the relationship with the (pre-Oedipal) mother, the dying, and possibly forgiving, words of Michel's mother – the only ones we hear her utter – have already gestured towards it. The absence of writing – Michel's diary has disappeared from view – would on a Lacanian reading strengthen this interpretation. If it also represents, in the more workaday perspective which is that of the fairy tale from Perrault to Capra ('they lived happily ever after and had lots of children'), the reproduction of the family unit, then Jacques's truancy has made possible for Michel a happy ending of a different, but not incompatible, kind. Curiously it is this film, in which biological fathers are absent (Michel's father, Jacques) and symbolic ones rejected (the inspector) or found wanting (the pickpocket played by Kassagi), that ultimately gives the most hopeful view of parenting in Bresson's work. As Jeanne moves from mother figure or substitute, the unanswered question is whether she is the agent or the instrument of Michel's redemption – is it by her or through her that his 'salvation', or in a non-theological perspective his escape from an all-devouring self-loathing, is accomplished? Between the Scylla of the aforementioned 'happy ending' and the Charybdis of a divine intervention at best unpalatable and at worst ruinously incomprehensible to non-believers, the undecidable turns out to provide the only answer. Neither a love story nor a parable of transcendental forgiveness, *Pickpocket* operates on the border between the human affection of Eros and the divine reach of Agape. If in its final scene Michel looks not only at but beyond Jeanne, that, after so many anguished and ambiguous looks and gazes in the film, figures the 'drôle de chemin' that he, and we the audience, have had to take.

Le Procès de Jeanne d'Arc

Bresson's next film – winner of the 1962 Jury Prize at Cannes – is, with the exception of *Affaires publiques*, his shortest, running for only sixty-five minutes. That conciseness is matched by the rapidity of the editing and dialogues, the latter, almost sticomythic in their starkness, based on the transcript of the historical Joan's trial[36] and centring on the forensic and spiritual joust between the institutional majesty of the chief judge (Cauchon) and Jeanne's recalcitrant and inspired individuality. This clash is conveyed less through the *mise en scène*, austere to the point of minimalism, than through the characters' different, and historically attested, use of language – Cauchon's portentous and menacing, Jeanne's sometimes pungently colloquial in a manner that seems to prefigure *Mouchette* (of a horse she allegedly took: 'Je ne l'ai pas pris, je l'ai payé. Et même je l'ai renvoyé. Le cheval ne valait rien').[37] Bresson's dialogues effectively give us a documentary reconstruction, cutting him off thereby from the interior monologues that have been an important part of his previous three films. Yet that does not mean that he is cutting himself off from the transcendental that is so fundamental to his work. His assertion that in this film he tried to 'trouver avec des mots historiques une vérité non historique'[38] (Bresson [1975] 1988: 128) suggests a dialectic between the material and the spiritual similar to that we have seen with particular force in *Journal*. He is also engaging, deliberately or not, in intertextual rivalry – what the

36 I use 'Joan' to refer to the historical character and 'Jeanne' for the central figure in Bresson's film.
37 'I didn't take it, I paid for it. I even sent it back. The horse was worthless.'
38 'to find with historical words a non-historical truth.'

American Gnostic/cabbalistic theorist Harold Bloom would call agon – with one of the silent cinema's greatest classics, Carl Theodor Dreyer's *La Passion de Jeanne d'Arc* of 1928. Bresson has written of the earlier film in somewhat deprecatory terms ('Faute de vrai, le public s'attache au faux. La façon expressionniste dont Mlle Falconetti lançait les yeux au ciel, dans le film de Dreyer, arrachait les larmes' (Bresson [1975] 1988: 1260)),[39] and most commentators on *Le Procès* have stressed its marked divergence from *La Passion*. I disagree with Sémolué's contention that in speaking of *Le Procès* one has to 'soit oublier *La Passion* pour n'envisager le film de Bresson que par rapport à son œuvre personnelle, soit ne plus songer qu'à comparer les deux *Jeanne d'Arc*'[40] (Sémolué 1993: 109). The contrast between the two films distils much that is central to Bresson's *œuvre personnelle*, beginning with *Le Procès*'s virtual absence of close-ups. The close-up is perceived by Andrew Sarris (Sarris 1971: 193) as a Protestant device, focusing as it does on the individual's struggle for salvation rather than on the institutional context in which it takes place – on, precisely, passion rather than process. The Dreyer film makes famously extensive and harrowing use of close-ups of Renée Falconetti, perhaps reminding us of the view that Joan was the first Protestant. It was to be Falconetti's first and last film role; the stress and anguish of making the film caused her to have a nervous breakdown, so that *La Passion* doubles as a documentary on its own making, appealing thereby to the sado-voyeuristic drives all but endemic to any attempt at filming the Joan of Arc story. At the same time, Falconetti's interpretation of Joan is nothing if not a performance, to use a word that is anathema to Bresson. Florence Carrez in *Le Procès* is as unlike Falconetti, or for that matter Jean Seberg in Preminger's *Saint Joan*, as one could imagine. Bresson has given us the anti-*Passion de Jeanne d'Arc*, so much so that he quarrelled bitterly with his cinematographer of

39 'If there is nothing true, the public becomes attached to the false. The expressionist way in which Mlle Falconetti cast her eyes heavenwards, in Dreyer's film, was tear-jerking.'

40 'Either forget about *La Passion* to focus on Bresson's film in the context of his personal *oeuvre*, or concentrate exclusively on comparing the two *Jeanne d'Arc*.'

ten years' standing, Léonce-Henry Burel, over his unwillingness to have Jeanne look up at the camera ('Bresson ... didn't want to have Joan look up because Dreyer had done that' (Burel 1998: 520)). Not only that; for Nicole Brenez writing in *Positif*, he has exercised a durable influence *a contrario* on the major French director subsequently to have made a film about Joan:

> Jeanne vient d'être livrée aux Anglais, on l'emmène à Rouen. Jacques Rivette introduit alors un intertitre. *'Le 24 mai 1431, à Rouen, après 4 mois de procès'* (*Jeanne la Pucelle I: les Prisons*, 1993). Il y a des images, en effet, qui n'ont pas besoin d'être refaites.[41] (Brenez 1996: 92)

The historicity of Bresson's Jeanne is guaranteed by the fidelity of the dialogues to the transcripts of the trial, emphasised by the introductory text displayed on screen at the beginning. The sense that Bresson's *modèles* quote their lines rather than expressing them – like in a very different context the characters in a Brecht play – is thus more powerful in *Le Procès* than anywhere else in his work. In one sense, then, the film could be described as a 'docu-drama', yet once we take its visual aspects into consideration that epithet becomes inappropriate in a way that goes beyond the stylistic. No likeness – portrait or engraving – of the historical Joan exists, so that no pictorial fidelity to her is even thinkable, and the physical environment of the film could be described as minimalist. To quote Sémolué, Bresson 'reste fidèle à l'atmosphère et aux faits historiques tout en éliminant le pittoresque, l'anecdotique'[42] (Sémolué 1993: 121), as the timeless quality of Jeanne's clothing – neither modern nor archaic – illustrates.

The film opens with Jeanne's mother reading her plea at the 1456 retrial. Most audiences will know that this led to Joan's rehabilitation, so that this brief introduction, like the title of *Un condamné* or Michel's diary and voice-over at the start of

---

41 'Jeanne has just been handed over to the English and is being taken to Rouen. Jacques Rivette then introduced an intertitle: "On 24 May 1431, in Rouen, after a four-month trial" (*Jeanne la Pucelle II: les Prisons*, 1993). Some images do not need reshooting.' (The French original has 1391 for 1431 – an obvious typo).

42 '[Bresson] remains faithful to the atmosphere and to historical facts while eliminating the picturesque and the anecdotal.'

Pickpocket, confirms that the film will in one sense at least end happily. We then witness five successive interrogations of Jeanne, in between which she returns to her cell. The disorder of the crowd causes Cauchon to decide to continue the interrogations in the cell, where she refuses to abandon the men's clothing that for her is the source of her strength. Resisting threats of torture, partly thanks to the moral support of the Dominican Isambart – almost her only earthly ally – she nonetheless briefly capitulates and signs a revocation, only to take it back and revert to men's clothing after an English lord has tried to abuse her sexually. She receives Communion for the last time and is led to the stake, clutching an improvised cross given her by an English soldier. As she burns, the two Dominicans hold up a much larger cross to her; she utters a final cry of 'Jésus!' and dies. We see the bare, charred stake alone at the end, in a manner similar to though starker than the cross at the end of *Journal*. (*Mouchette*, five years later, will be Bresson's third film to conclude with the disappearance of the main character's body.)

During the cell scenes, Jeanne is regularly spied upon through a hole in the door by Cauchon and her English captors, notably Warwick.[43] The French word for such a spy-hole is 'judas', and the spying episodes act as a fairly obvious reminder of the treachery that has delivered Jeanne into the hands of her enemies. Beyond this, they also carry an unmistakable sadistic charge reinforced by the muttered imputations about Jeanne's virginity and sexuality. Marina Warner argues that it was 'the diabolical character of her cross-dressing' (Warner 1996: 29) that was primarily responsible for her condemnation. Some considerable time before the concept of gender had ventured outside the world of linguistics, 'Joan was using male apparel to appear sexless, rather than male, to appear not-female, rather than female' (Warner, 1996: 27) – a wilful stepping outside the defining binary antitheses of sexuality that pre-dates those other celebrated 'strategic virgins' Queen

43 No character apart from Jeanne is referred to by name within the diegesis of the film. Prior historical knowledge or consultation of works such as those by Sémolué or Arnaud is necessary in order to identify them. It is as if Bresson had eschewed proper names the better to focus his film upon Jeanne.

Elizabeth I and Simone Weil. Bresson's rejection of acting and performance doubtless explains why Florence Carrez is better able to embody this threatening asexuality than the other cinematic Joans. Jean Seberg and Sandrine Bonnaire (Joan in the two Rivette films) bring with them quite strongly sexual personae from their previous work, while Falconetti's page-boy crop and all too real tears carry a powerful androgynous charge. In the Bresson film, the English lord's assault becomes the logical culmination of what has gone before – the attempt at imposing upon Jeanne a sexed identity her whole life and bearing refuse. The virginity exalted by the Church in the more passive figure of Mary becomes menacing when allied with the combativeness of the Church Militant, and something like a visual or discursive rape is required to neutralise that menace. Bresson's camera as it gazes through the spyhole at the sobbing Jeanne inevitably tends to draw the spectator into an identification with its perspective, an identification troubled and inverted when we see the eye in close-up from the other side of the cell door, as it were watching our own gaze. The visual sadism of *Le Procès* is more restrained and self-reflective than that of *La Passion*, but none the less disturbing for that.

Jean-Pierre Oudart, in a *Cahiers du cinéma* piece that became extremely influential in spectatorship theory, makes great claims for *Le Procès*'s laying bare of the mechanisms of spectator identification in what he calls, after Bresson and in opposition to 'cinema', 'la cinématographie'. Oudart was subsequently to describe 'le rapport sadien entre le metteur en scène et ses actrices' as 'le refoulé de la fiction bressonienne'[44] (Oudart 1972: 88) – this refers to *Quatre nuits d'un rêveur*, but as we have just seen is no less applicable to *Le Procès*. Oudart is not necessarily referring here solely to the biographical Robert Bresson's attitude towards his *modèles*, for the problematic within which he is working stresses the cinematographic process, and within it the role of 'director' and 'actor', as above all constructed. It is at the level of camera positioning and the identificatory possibilities this enables for or forces upon the spectator, rather than within

44 'The Sadean relationship between the director and his actresses [is] the repressed of the Bressonian fiction.'

Bresson-the-man's psyche, that Oudart's 'rapport sadien' is to be found – perhaps a convenient way of having one's referential cake and eating it.

Oudart's article does not so much analyse spectator positioning within *Le Procès* as use the film to articulate a view of filmic space grounded in the concept of 'suture', after the surgical term for stitching together the two edges of a wound. (The sexual, sadistic and medicalising overtones of the term perhaps make it peculiarly appropriate in connection with a film about Joan of Arc.) For Oudart, any filmic field implies the existence of an absent character in the place of the 'fourth side' of the image, as it were 'between' the image on screen and the spectator in the cinema. The filmic field is thus articulated around the point of view of this (non-existent) character, called by Oudart 'l'Absent', posited by the spectator's 'imaginaire' (Oudart 1972: 37). This in turn means that any totalising view of the image as complete in itself, or of the spectator as occupying a fixed and immutable position in relation to the signifying chain of images, is a delusion. Oudart's use of the term 'imaginaire' stems from Lacanian psychoanalysis, for which it denotes the period of pre-Oedipal plenitude before the infant's recognition of sexual difference and acquisition of language. Lacan's work, still very important in film studies, was, along with the Marxism of Louis Althusser, the dominant paradigm for *Cahiers* in the 1970s, and exercised immense influence in the same period on the British journal *Screen*, in which Oudart's piece was translated along with a critical commentary by Stephen Heath (reproduced in Heath 1981). This theoretical tendency, deriving from the cultural upheaval of May 1968, was concerned above all to contest the primacy of realism in political film-making, stressing rather the need to *"faire politiquement des films politiques"*[45] (Godard and Gorin: quoted in Cerisuelo 1989: 152). The work of Godard, Straub and Huillet, the Japanese Oshima was revolutionary less because of its subject-matter or the overt sympathies it might express than through the manner in which it broke apart the 'imaginary' (in a Lacanian sense) fullness of the spectator's

45 'to make political films in a political way.'

identification with the images on screen, thereby emphasising that 'ce n'est pas une image juste, c'est juste une image'[46] (an intertitle from Godard/the Dziga–Vertov group's *Vent d'Est*).

Le Procès's importance, for Oudart, resides in its laying bare – what would later have been described as its deconstruction – of the mechanisms of suture which represent the spectator's relation to cinematographic discourse. It is as though the film's 'subject' were not the trial of Joan at all, but rather the viewing 'subject' postulated by its articulations. The tone of Oudart's piece, which extols *Le Procès* and disparages *Balthazar*, tends to the apodictic and essentialist, for which it is criticised by Stephen Heath:

> The problem is the evaluation, with behind that the status accorded suture in the description given ... The system of the suture seems in this context to be something of an essence of cinema, its veritable 'passion' (note here the manner in which the presence or absence of a feature like depth of field can provide Oudart with an immediate criterion for judgement: the use of images without depth in modern cinema hides the fundamental movement of cinema; *Balthazar* is characterised by an irritating abandon of all depth of field; and so on). (Heath 1981: 91)

I have dwelt upon Oudart's piece and Heath's criticism of it because it marks probably the major impact Bresson's work has had upon the wider development of film theory, and also because any reader coming to it in expectation of an improved grasp of *Le Procès* is likely to be somewhat bemused. Bresson's film functions for Oudart precisely as a pre-text, an exemplar to be gestured towards; for an analysis of how suture functions at once to construct and to deconstruct the film's space, we have to turn to Philippe Arnaud. As in *Un condamné*, where the topography of the prison is never available to us as a whole, so here the courtroom is never shown in its entirety as it is in the establishing shot of classic 'courtroom drama'. This absence 'nous signifie cette hétérogénéité radicale entre Jeanne et ses juges: comme si, en effet, ils n'étaient pas du même monde'.[47] Culturally, linguisti-

46 'it is not a just/accurate image, it is just an image.'
47 'signifies to us the radical heterogeneity between Jeanne and her judges: as though, indeed, they were not of the same world.'

cally, sociologically, spiritually this is self-evident; Bresson's film articulates it not through performance or vocal inflection (Jeanne does not speak with an accent different to her judges), but through its construction of cinematographic space.[48] The overlapping of gazes in the five interrogation scenes sutures, as Oudart puts it, the spectator into the heterogeneity of the film, by way of 'une série de relais discrets, qui régentent strictement et l'affrontement de Jeanne et des juges, et la place du spectateur'[49] (Arnaud 1986: 103). There is a helpful diagram (Arnaud 1986: 102) illustrating the 'relais' in question. Arnaud shows how the viewing-subject positions successively produced by the film impart their rhythm to the interrogation scenes, so that it is the spectator who is in a very real sense called into question.

Is there a focal point for audience identification within these scenes? What has been said hitherto would seem to suggest not, but Arnaud draws attention to the character of Isambart, the young Dominican whose glances and gestures offer periodic encouragement and support to Jeanne. Isambart is situated 'à une place dans la salle du tribunal proche de la nôtre, celle que nous assigne le croisement des deux axes principaux'[50] (Arnaud 1986: 103). This implies that the spectators, rather than being detached observers as the film's quasi-documentary style may seem to imply, are placed in some sense 'with' Jeanne, willing her on through Isambart's surreptitious signals. The status of these, and indeed of Isambart himself, is curiously equivocal. He is referred to (as 'Ysambard') in the transcript of the trial, but with no suggestion of particular benevolence towards or complicity with Joan, though at the rehabilitation he was an eloquent witness on her behalf. It is almost as if Bresson were providing the spectator with a sympathetic representative or surrogate – 'notre délégué',[51] to quote Sémolué (Sémolué 1993: 119) – during Jeanne's public

48 It is worth pointing out that Sitney criticises Oudart for ignoring the particular importance of verbal exchanges in Le Procès (Sitney, 1998: 146).
49 'a series of discrete relays which strictly control both Jeanne's confrontation with her judges and the place of the spectator.'
50 'in a place in the courtroom close to ours, the place assigned to us by the crossing of the two main axes.'
51 'our delegate.'

ordeal, to offset the sadistic voyeurism at work in the cell scenes.

The film's final scene breaks with what has gone before, for it opens with a tracking-shot – one of the very few in the film, and an echo of her mother's movement in the prologue (Sémolué 1993: 119) – depicting Jeanne's feet shuffling towards the stake. Once she has been bound to the stake and the faggots have been lit, shot/reverse-shot comes back into play, this time between the Dominicans who hold up the large metal cross and the smoke that conceals and stifles Jeanne. The sadism latent in these shots is held at bay – by the cross, crushing emblem of ecclesiastical majesty but also sign of salvation, as by the invisibility of Jeanne's agonising body. Time – of fundamental importance in this film grounded in history and rhythmed by interrogation – here seems suspended, and it comes as no surprise that when the smoke lifts Jeanne's body has altogether disappeared. Drum-rolls echoing those at the beginning bring the film to a close.

The following year (1963), Bresson went to Rome to work on a projected version of *La Genèse*, to be produced by Dino De Laurentiis. It was predictable that cooperation with a figure so strongly associated with popular and epic cinema would not be easy, and Bresson soon returned to France in disgruntlement. He was not to film an expressly religious or historical subject again; *Lancelot du lac*, for all its medieval 'realism', deals with myth rather than history. Henceforth, his relationship with the life of the spirit and the texts in which it is articulated was to be a more overtly secular, though no less intense, one.

References

Arnaud, Philippe (1986), *Robert Bresson*, Paris, Cahiers du Cinéma.

Barthes, Roland (1973), *Le Plaisir du texte*, Paris, Seuil.

Bazin, André (1997), 'Un Condamné à mort s'est échappé', in *Robert Bresson: Éloge*, Milan and Paris, Mazzotta/Cinémathèque française.

Bennington, Geoffrey (1988), *Lyotard: Writing the Event*, Manchester, Manchester University Press.

Bordwell, David (1985), *Narration in Fiction Film*, London, Methuen.

Brenez, Nicole, (1996) '"Approche inhabituelle des corps": Bresson avec Jean Eustache, Philippe Garrel et Monte Hellman', *Positif*, no. 430.

Bresson, Robert ([1975] 1988), *Notes sur le cinématographe*, Paris, Gallimard.
Burch, Noël (1969), *Praxis du cinéma*, Paris, Gallimard.
Buret, Léonce-Henry (1998), in James Quandt (ed.), *Robert Bresson*, Cinematheque Ontario, Toronto.
Cahiers du cinéma, February 1989.
Cerisuelo, Marc (1989), *Jean-Luc Godard*, Paris, Quatre-Vents.
Chion, Michel (1992), *Le Son au cinéma*, Paris, Cahiers du cinéma.
Cinéma 63, no. 73.
Deleuze, Gilles (1983), *Cinéma 1: L'Image–mouvement*, Paris, Minuit.
Estève, Michel (1983), *Robert Bresson: la passion du cinématographe*, Paris, Albatros.
Ferrero, Adelio (1976), *Robert Bresson*, Florence, La Nuova Italia.
Freud, Sigmund ([1900] 1976), *The Interpretation of Dreams*, Harmondsworth, Pelican.
Heath, Stephen (1981), *Questions of Cinema*, London, BFI/Macmillan.
Herbert, George ([c. 1635] 1994), *The Works of George Herbert*, Ware, Wordsworth.
Kline, T. Jefferson (1992), *Screening the Text: Intertextuality in French New Wave Cinema*, Baltimore, Johns Hopkins University Press.
Leterrier, François (1956), 'Robert Bresson l'insaissible', *Cahiers du cinéma*, 66: 34–6.
Lindeperg, Sylvie (1996), *Les Écrans de l'ombre*, Paris, CNRS.
Malle, Louis (1997), '*Pickpocket*', in *Robert Bresson: Éloge*, Milan/Paris, Mazzotta/ Cinémathèque française.
Millar, Daniel (1962), '*Pickpocket*', in I. Cameron (ed.), *The Films of Robert Bresson*, London, Studio Vista.
Noguera, Rui (1998), 'Burel and Bresson', in James Quandt (ed.), *Robert Bresson*, Cinematheque Ontario, Toronto.
Oudart, Jean-Pierre (1969), 'La Suture', *Cahiers du cinéma*, no. 211.
Oudart, Jean-Pierre (1972), 'Le Hors-champ de l'auteur', *Cahiers du cinéma*, nos. 236–7.
Prédal, René (1992), *Robert Bresson: l'aventure intérieure*, *L'Avant-scène cinéma*, nos. 408–9.
Quandt, James (ed.), *Robert Bresson*, Cinematheque Ontario, Toronto.
Reader, Keith (1998), '"D'où cela vient-il?": notes on three films by Robert Bresson', in James Quandt (ed.), *Robert Bresson*, Cinematheque Ontario, Toronto.
Salles Gomes, P. E. (1957), *Jean Vigo*, Paris, Seuil.
Sarris, Andrew (1971), *Confessions of a Cultist*, New York, Simon and Schuster.
Sartre, Jean-Paul (1949), *La Mort dans l'âme*, Paris, Gallimard.
Sémolué, Jean (1993), *Bresson ou l'acte pur des métamorphoses*, Paris, Flammarion.
Sitney, P. Adams (1998), 'Cinematography vs. the Cinema: Bresson's Figures', in James Quandt (ed.), *Robert Bresson*, Cinematheque Ontario, Toronto.
Sontag, Susan (1964), 'Spiritual Style in the Films of Robert Bresson', in James Quandt (ed.), *Robert Bresson*, Cinematheque Ontario, Toronto.
Truffaut, François (1975), *Les Films de ma vie*, Paris, Flammarion.
Truffaut, François and Latil-Le Dantec, Mireille (1997), 'Entretien sur Robert Bresson', in *Robert Bresson: Hommage*, Milan and Paris, Mazzotta/ Cinémathèque française.
Warner, Marina (1996), *Joan of Arc*, Evesham, Arthur James.

1 *Affaires publiques* (1934): Bresson's first, and only, comic film

2 Hell hath no fury ... Maria Casarès as Hélène in *Les Dames du Bois de Boulogne* (1945)

3 The priest's agony soothed in *Journal d' un curé de campagne* (1951)

4 Jost poised for escape in *Un condamné à mort s' est échappé* (1956)

73

5 Joan in *Le Procès de Jeanne d' Arc* (1962)

6 *Mouchette* (1967): Mouchette's moment of liberation on the dodgems

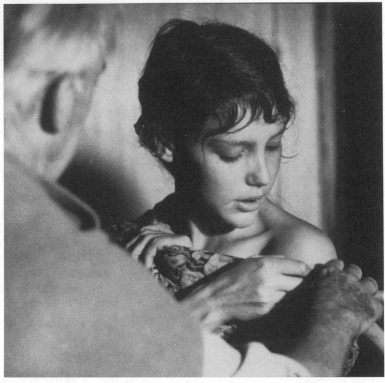

7 Marie/Anne Wiazemsky with Bresson on the set of *Au hasard Balthazar* (1966)

8 The *femme douce* (Dominique Sanda) runs towards her husband (1969)

9 Courtly love in *Lancelot du lac* (1974)

4

The last black-and-white films:
Au hasard Balthazar and *Mouchette*

Au hasard Balthazar

The Franco-Swedish coproduction *Au hasard Balthazar* (herein-after *Balthazar*), released in 1966, is the most complex and baffling, but also for a great many critics (of whom I am one) the most thoroughly 'Bressonian', of its maker's works. That it was shown out of competition at Cannes seems entirely appropriate, for to quote the unreconstructedly *auteurist* words of Marguerite Duras: 'C'est peut-être le film que j'ai vu qui correspond le plus à une création solitaire, donc à la création proprement dite'[1] (Duras, 1997: 49). *Balthazar* differs from the films that went before it in a number of ways. It foregoes linear narrative in favour of a criss-crossing amalgam of characters and their trajectories, whose course and motivation are often quite difficult to understand at a first viewing. It includes a number of moments of quiet humour, such as the pompous conversation of the artists riding on Balthazar and his companion, Arnold's lugubrious final apostro-phising of the milestone and the lamppost or the reaction of the peasant after Balthazar has overturned his cart – the latter unremarked by critics, but adroitly picked up by Bill Forsyth in his Channel 4 Movie Masterclass programme on the film. It is set in a provincial France (the Pyrenees) more recognisably contemporary than the world of the earlier films. Leather jackets, mopeds,

---

1 'It is perhaps of all the films I have seen the one that most corresponds to solitary creation, and thus to creation in the true sense of the word.'

transistor radios, teeth-grittingly awful French rock music all make their appearance, and the brawl sequence in which Gérard smashes up the village bar while couples dance blithely away is the most visceral piece of cinema Bresson had given us hitherto. One sub-plot – the village schoolmaster's acquisition, development and eventual loss of the land he farms – implicitly refers to the large-scale rationalisation of agriculture in the France of the time and the upheavals it caused, while the schoolmaster himself, proud above all of his self-education through reading, clearly represents the French tradition of the *école laïque* which since the secularisation of state education in 1881 has traditionally opposed itself to the Catholic Church. (A vestige of this persists in the schoolmaster's turning away from the priest who comes to his deathbed.) Bresson is scarcely the first film-maker to whom one would turn for portrayal or analysis of French society, but *Balthazar* is more than it might appear a film of its time.

Its most striking innovation is of course the use of a donkey as the 'central character'. Outside the cartoon, lead roles for animals have by and large been confined to action dramas for children, of the *Lassie* or *Rin-Tin-Tin* variety. More than thirty years after *Balthazar*, I know of no film that has made such profound or audacious use of an animal protagonist. This is not, of course, to everybody's taste – not to mine the first time I saw the film, nor to that of Bresson's stalwart *Positif* enemy Robert Benayoun who waxes sarcastic about 'le pauvre petit nanâne'[2] (Benayoun 1966: 82). Bresson himself adopts an unabashedly anthropomorphic attitude towards the donkey, speaking of how 'l'âne a dans la vie les mêmes étapes que l'homme', culminating in 'la période mystique qui précède la mort'[3] (Godard and Delahaye 1966: 30). Balthazar's name – derived apparently from a medieval motto of the Counts of Les Baux in Provence, but also evoking the Three Wise Men – works to endow him with a perhaps unexpected nobility. The religious overtones of the beast that carried Christ are made explicit in one of the film's final images, when Balthazar

2 'the poor dear little donkey.'
3 'the donkey goes through the same stages of life as man ... the mystic period before death.'

is shown laden with a shrine in a procession. Other intertexts often cited include Watteau's painting *Gilles*, which features a donkey observing calmly in the background, and Dostoevsky's *The Idiot*, in Chapter Five of which Myshkin relates how the braying of a donkey in the market-place at Bâle caused his depression to disappear. We may also be reminded by the scenes in which Balthazar is mistreated that Nietzsche's final breakdown was precipitated by the savage beating of a carthorse in a Turin street; he threw his arms around the animal's neck and burst into tears, never again to utter a word.

The donkey as scapegoat, as observer, as literal or metaphorical bearer of the divine – these connotations figure prominently in European culture and give the presence of Balthazar much of its force. They also help – *pace* Benayoun – to avoid any suspicion of sentimentality, at least once Balthazar is fully grown. In the earlier sequences, where he is still a baby, such implications are undercut by the narrative irony that is one of the film's structuring devices – first in the opening sequence, when Jacques and his sister are told by their father that it is impossible for them to have Balthazar only to be seen taking him home immediately afterwards, and later when Jacques, returning home with his family at the end of their holiday, says: 'A l'année prochaine',[4] followed by a reverse shot of Balthazar as though to suggest that it is to the donkey, not Marie, that these words are addressed. This shot, whose charm is inseparable from its slight incongruity, already places Balthazar where he will always be, at the centre of the film's overlapping action. Godard, in a lengthy *Cahiers* interview with Bresson which suggests how important the film was immediately perceived to be, contrasted *Balthazar* to Bresson's previous work: 'vos autres films étaient des lignes droites, et ... celui-ci est plutôt fait ... de cercles concentriques qui se recoupent les uns les autres'[5] (Godard and Delahaye 1966: 31). This echoes the Pascalian description of God as 'une sphère infinie dont le centre est partout, la circonférence nulle part'[6] (Pascal [1670] 1976: 65), and the omnipresent centre in this film can only be Balthazar. Lindley Hanlon invokes Pascal's view of animal time, foregrounding its 'perception of the novelty of each instant', (Hanlon 1986: 96), as a possible analogy for *Balthazar*'s narrative fragmentation, while for Nick Browne, the narrator 'represents himself in the text, allegorically, as the eye of Balthazar' (Browne 1977: 30). Thus, between film-maker, narrator, the animal and the divine a complex and ineffable relationship is set up that provides the film with its curiously shifting consistency.

The donkey that plays Balthazar (if that is the right verb to use) proved no more accommodating than many of Bresson's other *modèles*, periodically irritating the director through his refusal to behave as 'asked'. It is interesting to learn that the scenes where Balthazar is performing in the circus were shot last, since Bresson did not want an already-trained donkey for the rest of the film; the distinction between actor and *modèle* is evidently as valid for animals as for human beings. That distinction may be called into question for a contemporary viewer of *Balthazar*, since Anne Wiazemsky (Marie) went on to work with Godard (*La Chinoise*, *One plus one/Sympathy with the Devil*) and Pasolini (*Pigsty*), while Jean-Claude Guilbert (Arnold), uniquely in Bresson's work, went on to play the very similar role of Arsène in *Mouchette*. Pierre Klossowski (the miserly grain merchant) is a well-known literary theorist and authority on Sade, though Bresson claimed not to have read his work.

Philippe Arnaud's summary of *Balthazar* takes more than seven pages of text, and is followed by a quotation from Robbe-Grillet which suggests strong similarities between the film and the formal changes wrought by Robbe-Grillet and his fellow *nouveaux romanciers* ('L'avènement du roman moderne est précisément lié à cette découverte: le réel est discontinu, formé d'éléments juxtaposés sans raison dont chacun est unique, d'autant plus difficiles à saisir qu'ils surgissent de façon sans cesse imprévue,

---

6 'an infinite sphere whose centre is everywhere and whose circumference is nowhere.'

hors de propos, aléatoire' (Robbe-Grillet 1984: 208)).[7] There is, nevertheless, comparatively little narrative ambiguity, *stricto sensu*, in *Balthazar*. The relationships between the two families at the beginning are not immediately obvious, but quickly become plainer, and on a second viewing at least it is clear that Jacques's father makes the land over to Marie's – the source of the subsequent ill-feeling between the two – because he is devastated by the death of his little daughter. The major narrative ambiguity concerns what happens to Marie at the end; we are told along with Jacques that she has gone away and will not be back, but more than that we never know. Yet compared to Antonioni's *L'Avventura* of 1960, in which Anna's disappearance remains utterly unexplained, or indeed to any number of *films noirs*, this is scarcely a major narrative obscurity. Uncertainty – Robbe-Grillet's 'discontinu' – arises in *Balthazar* much more at the level of motivation, and then only if we feel called upon to make a choice between different 'explanations'. Why does the baker's wife lavish gifts on the ungrateful Gérard? Is she merely anxious to keep his undoubted energy on her side, is he the son she has never had, is there perhaps a sexual relationship, actual or potential? We can, of course, answer 'yes' to some or all of these questions (there is no incompatibility between them). We can, on the other hand, follow Balthazar's example and decline to answer or even ask any of them, contenting ourselves with the wisdom of contemplation and the occasional raucous bray of anguish or derision. Most spectators will probably find themselves oscillating between these two modes of viewing, between filling in the film's gaps and leaving its sense(s) to speak through them, so that *Balthazar*'s challenge – the donkey's and the film's – to our ways of viewing becomes an integral part of its meaning. In this sense, and despite (or perhaps because of) Bresson's general disinclination to say much about the audience for which his films aim, it can be said of him, as Deleuze says of Hitchcock, that he 'ne conçoit plus la

7 'The advent of the modern novel is precisely linked to this discovery: the real is discontinuous, made up of elements juxtaposed without reason each of which is unique, and all the harder to grasp since their appearance is never predictable but always beside the point, a matter of chance.'

constitution d'un film en fonction de deux termes, le metteur en scène, et le film à faire, mais en fonction de trois: le metteur en scène, le film, et le public qui doit entrer dans le film'[8] (Deleuze 1983: 272).

While I have less space at my disposal than Arnaud, I shall still give a fairly extensive summary of the plot of *Balthazar*, for its complexity of detail means that much is likely to be missed on a first viewing at any rate. The film opens with the slow movement from Schubert's penultimate piano sonata (D959), interrupted by Balthazar's braying. The berceuse-like melody recurs in the film at moments that hark back to the childhood happiness and tranquillity of its opening sequence – feelings rapidly disrupted by the fatal illness of Jacques's sister and not, it would seem, to be recaptured thereafter. Schubert's sonata, in one of the most extraordinary slow movements of the classical piano repertoire, opposes to its opening berceuse a tempestuous middle sequence in which the melody breaks apart and the harmonies become disjointed. Balthazar's braying on the film soundtrack takes the place of that sequence, preserving the music's lyricism and so to speak protecting it from itself much as he is later to function as a talisman of bliss long gone for Jacques and Marie. The end of the Schubert slow movement brings back the berceuse, but only after a slow transitional sequence evocative of hesitancy and pain. We shall see that it is possible to read the end of Bresson's film in a very similar way.

The baby donkey is 'baptised' by the children, who play with him in the straw. Jacques carves his name along with Marie's on a bench before the family leave, the signal for a brutal transition to Balthazar being whipped, shod and harnessed to begin his 'adult' life as a working donkey. The cart he is drawing overturns and the farmer denounces Balthazar to a group of peasants who pursue him armed with pitchforks – a humorous image, as Bill Forsyth has pointed out, but also in its way a frightening one, reminiscent of the diabolisation of animals that could lead in the Middle Ages

8 '[he] no longer conceives of a film as structured around two terms, the director and the film to be made, but around three: the director, the film and the audience that has to enter into the film.'

to their being tried and put to death. Balthazar takes to his heels and finds himself back in his youthful home, the first of the number of would-be returns to childhood that punctuate the film. Marie's father, the schoolteacher, explains to her that the fields he has so strenuously cultivated do not in fact belong to the family – the source of the anxiety expressed in his constant striding through those fields calling for his daughter. Already we become aware that *Balthazar* is structured musically or poetically as much as narratively, at the level of units or themes like the Schubert sonata or the schoolmaster's repeated cries of 'Marie!'

The next episode introduces us to Gérard and his blouson-clad accomplices, seen spilling oil on the road so as to cause not one, but two cars successively to crash. Characters in this scene are depicted from the waist down, as if to suggest that their bodies obey impulses divorced from their hearts or minds – a device to be used repeatedly in *Lancelot du lac* and *Le Diable probablement*. Two Bresson devices familiar from his earlier work are also used to telling effect. Key actions take place off-screen (the second car crash here, like the buying of the young Balthazar earlier or the killing of the guard in *Un condamné*); and the importance of repetition in the *jouissance* of the forbidden is stressed. Michel's thieving in *Pickpocket* is the most striking example of the last-named, but Gérard and his gang also, we are made to feel, enjoy the fact that their vandalistic action is repeated almost as much as the action itself. Gérard's often gratuitous violence thus becomes an expression of Thanatos – the Freudian death-wish issuing in endless repetition – though the death, or perhaps deaths, in which it results will not include his own.

Gérard's gang mock Balthazar ('C'est chouette, un âne. – Rapide. – Moderne'), in tones later to be reprised more seriously by Marie's father ('Cet âne est rétrograde et ridicule').[9] The donkey is associated with an earlier, more innocent and less swift-moving period in the development of the French countryside as well as that of the film's central characters. Marie is spied upon by Gérard and his friends in the barn bedecking Balthazar with flowers,

9 'Donkeys are cool. – Speedy. – Modern' ... 'This donkey is reactionary and ridiculous.'

which prompts Gérard to speculate: 'Elle peut l'aimer d'amour et lui aussi'.[10] *A Midsummer Night's Dream* suggests, albeit in burlesque mode, the possible sexual connotations of the donkey. Bresson's scene is moving because it captures a nascent sexuality which the childhood friendship between young woman and donkey and the hieratic garlanding endow, however transiently, with innocence. Gérard's move to take Marie's hand immediately afterwards marks the beginning of the end of her innocence just as the first blow dealt to Balthazar has done for his.

Marie is later to tell her mother that she does whatever Gérard tells her to and would kill herself if he asked her – a depth of self-abnegation that marks her out as the most extreme, even pathological, example of the *femme douce* in Bresson's work. Agnès's meekness is in the end her, and Jean's, greatest strength, as is Jeanne's for Michel; Jeanne d'Arc's makes her a saint; the unnamed heroine of *Une femme douce* will proffer resistance along with her gentleness; the grey-haired woman – also unnamed – in *L'Argent* may ensure Yvon's salvation by her self-sacrifice. There is no indication that Gérard is in any sense redeemed, or even affected, by Marie's prostration before him. Godard's description of her as 'si j'ose dire, un autre âne'[11] (Godard and Delahaye 1966: 30) is, however, less purely cynical than it may appear. The closeness of the identification between Marie and Balthazar, apparent from the beginning and perhaps strongest in the garlanding scene, means that as the film unfolds he will take her burden upon himself along with all the rest. A donkey cannot, of course, take on a burden other than in the most literal physical sense; but the intensely material spirituality of the film works, via a kind of 'poetic realism', to reactivate the Christian metaphorical sense of the term, so that by the time we, along with Balthazar, reach the end it will seem far from incongruous that he is in some sense sacrificing himself for her.

Jacques returns and, as he will never cease to do, reaffirms his unchanging love for Marie, who cannot be sure that she loves him. Gérard becomes Balthazar's 'master', using him to deliver bread

10 'She may be really in love with him and he with her.'
11 'if I dare say so, a second donkey.'

and mistreating him much as he does the besotted and helpless
Marie. The drunken Arnold appears to be suspected of a murder
which, though we are never given any details of it, may equally
well have been committed by Gérard. A sequence telescoping the
seasons together shows Balthazar neglected outside the shack
where Gérard and Marie are closeted. Arnold takes him away just
as he is about to be put down, and comments poetically upon his
recovery ('La route devait le tuer, elle l'a guéri').[12] Terrified that he
may have committed murder in a drunken frenzy, Arnold swears
never to drink again; the next shot shows him swigging himself
into near insensibility in a café.

Balthazar is (presumably) sold to a travelling zoo and circus,
where we see him successively gazing at, and being gazed at by, a
lion, a polar bear, a monkey and an elephant. The importance of
the gaze in spectator theory is copiously documented, but usually
– following Laura Mulvey – in a gendered context clearly inappli-
cable here. The scene is generally agreed to be at once moving and
amusing (if we can forget the horrible conditions in which such
animals are often kept), but in ways and for reasons which remain
difficult to articulate. Arnaud observes that 'son malaise tient à ce
qu'il est impossible d'en domestiquer l'effet en lui conférant un
attribut' – a 'suspension de tout sens possible' that 'redistribue sa
force sur tout le reste du film'[13] (Arnaud 1986: 59). The most
celebrated cinematic experiment with editing, carried out by the
Russian Lev Kuleshov, emphasised the importance of montage in
the production of meaning. By placing the same shot of a face in a
variety of different contexts, Kuleshov was able to show that 'the
expression perceived on an actor's face – grief, joy, etc. – is
determined by the shots which precede and follow it' (Wollen
1970: 40). Lindley Hanlon's discussion of the film alludes to the
Kuleshov effect, 'used by Bresson to suggest moral reactions on
the part of Balthazar' (Hanlon, 1986: 82). But Balthazar is not an
'actor', and the zoo scene more than any other known to me in

---

12 'The road was meant to kill him, it has cured him.'
13 'it has an uneasy quality because it is impossible to tame its effect by conferring
   an attribute upon it – a suspension of any possible sense that redistributes its
   force throughout the rest of the film.'

western cinema at least generates what might be called an 'anti-Kuleshov effect', in which the montage of the animals' gazes *un*determines the 'expression perceived', making it impossible, as Arnaud says, to assign a sense to it. The elusiveness of the scene distils that inscribed within the film as a whole by Balthazar's central role, as a 'witness' who cannot properly speaking be one.

Balthazar performs in the circus until taken away once more by Arnold, who is summoned to the police station not to be charged with murder but to be told that he has inherited a fortune. He gets drunk at the celebration in the village café and falls from Balthazar's back to his death. Balthazar is bought by the grain merchant, who is niggardly with his food and treats him harshly. Marie arrives distressed at his door one stormy night, determined to break with Gérard. The merchant's avarice and cynicism ('J'aime l'argent, je déteste la mort')[14] seem to win over Marie, less surprisingly perhaps than many think; it is not, after all, difficult to imagine an older, materially successful Gérard proffering similar remarks. She spends the night with him. Her parents take Balthazar back, after an initial refusal, in settlement of an old debt; Marie and he are once again under the same roof. Jacques and Marie are together for the last time, Jacques eager to marry, Marie captured by the spirit of the times ('le mariage, c'est périmé')[15] and now bored by her childhood sweetheart. She contrasts his sentimental nostalgia with her own hardness of heart ('Je n'ai plus de tendresse, plus de cœur. Je suis insensible'),[16] yet says in Balthazar's presence, as if pronouncing a vow, that she will love Jacques ('Je l'aimerai, je l'aimerai').[17]

Gérard and his gang find Marie, beat her, strip her and lock her in a disused building, where she is seen, in perhaps the most prurient shot in Bresson's work, naked and sobbing. She leaves for an unknown destination, never to return. Her father dies. Gérard and accomplices want to borrow Balthazar, but Marie's mother refuses, saying that he is all she has 'et puis c'est un

14 'I love money, I hate death.'
15 'marriage is out of date.'
16 'I have no tenderness and no heart left. I am insensitive.'
17 'I shall love him, I shall love him.'

saint'.[18] Why does this remark, to me at least, appear deeply moving rather than the theological absurdity it so patently is? Partly perhaps because the bleakness of what has preceded it – two deaths and a disappearance – has been so unrelieved that some kind of sanctity seems called for to redress it; partly because Balthazar appears untouched by the evils he has witnessed; partly because his meekness has some kind of effect even on those who treat him most badly, except of course for Gérard – Arnold is bending to embrace him when he falls to his death, even the grain merchant fleetingly caresses him. Gérard steals Balthazar by night and loads him with consumer goods to smuggle into Spain, including gold and perfume (= frankincense) in an allusion to the Three Wise Men. They are spotted by armed police; Balthazar is shot and Gérard flees. In the morning, Balthazar, bleeding from his wound, hears the bells of a passing flock of sheep who surround him, a lamb prominent in the foreground, as he dies to the final recurrence of the Schubert melody.

Balthazar's death has given rise to a variety of commentaries, many of them presenting it as the tragic culmination of a film from which God is absent and whose pessimism is more marked than in any of Bresson's previous works. Thus, for *France Soir*'s anonymous critic 'des moutons plus curieux que compatissants se groupent autour de l'âne moribond et le film s'achève sur cette image magnifique et désespérée[19] (*France Soir* 1966). These remarks, like scattered references to Balthazar's 'agony', seem to me based on a misreading of the final sequence. 'Agony' in the strict etymological sense refers to the battle or struggle against death – surely an inappropriate term for the tranquil manner in which Balthazar lies down to die. The sheep are in one sense realistic (sheep are farmed in the French Pyrenees), but their sudden appearance in such numbers, accompanied by the tolling of their bells, surely invites us to read it in a biblical light that is anything but despairing. Godard in *Weekend*, made the year after Bresson's film, makes mocking use of the miraculous appearance

18 'and then he's a saint.'
19 'sheep who are inquisitive rather than compassionate gather round the dying donkey, and the film ends on this magnificent and despairing image.'

of sheep, as Buñuel had done in *The Exterminating Angel* of 1962 – intertexts for a view of *Balthazar*'s sheep that goes beyond the naturalistic. Further support for this is provided by the presence of the lamb (implausibly, there is only one), which may evoke the analogy between the Lamb of God who takes away the sins of the world and Balthazar suggested by Sémolué's observation that 'la mort de l'âne est comme une compensation au sadisme et à la folie des hommes'[20] (Sémolué 1983: 30). Bresson's lamb is also reminiscent of the Lamb of God at the foot of the Cross in Matthias Grünewald's magnificent *Issenheim Altarpiece* of 1516, to be found in the Unterlinden Museum in Colmar. Grünewald's lamb peers up at the stark figure of the crucified Christ with a curiosity from which compassion is certainly not absent, holding the Cross under its raised front leg while blood squirts from a wound in its chest into a chalice. Distress and hope are certainly here in all but equal measure, along with something else – a something else suggested by the lamb's almost nonchalant demeanour and its suggestion of a dog or cat urinating, a something else there earlier in *Balthazar* in the overturning of the peasant's cart and the 'recognition' scene in the zoo, a something else that stems from a playing with the uneasy anthropomorphism we are bound to bring to any allegorical use of an animal. Grünewald's lamb lightens the sombre canvas not only through its white fleece, but because it is at once a biological lamb utterly innocent of good and evil and the Lamb of God all-knowing of both, and the play between these two representations in one makes any unequivocal response to it, for me at least, extremely difficult.

Such play, we have seen, is also present in *Balthazar*, suggesting that its ending is what Anne Wiazemsky described to me as a 'Dostoevskyan' one, in which despair and salvation coexist and the oscillation between them imparts to the sequence a kind of temporality different from what we have encountered earlier in the film. This is partly because of its circularity, which brings Balthazar back to the mountains where he was born – back,

20 'the donkey's death is by way of a compensation for the sadism and folly of men.'

therefore, to a setting of innocence in a manner that has been tragically impossible for Marie. It is also because, like many human death scenes (we may think of the end of *Mouchette*), it suggests something like a temporal rite of passage. Animals in Catholic theology – even saintly ones – do not have souls and thus cannot partake of eternity. Yet the serenity of the Schubert slow movement, and the gentleness of its punctuation by the sheep's bells rather than the harsh braying we have heard earlier, reinforce the sense that Balthazar's dying, if not his death, brings his life back upon itself and near to a kind of eternity. This is what for me justifies Mirella Jona Affron's assertion that 'Balthazar dies in glory' (Affron 1998: 170). Against all expectations and many readings, the ending of *Au hasard Balthazar* redeems the chance in the film's title through a wager of positively Pascalian daring.

Mouchette

Godard, in a characteristically pre-postmodern *Cahiers* article ('Testament') juxtaposing confected Bressonian remarks with citations from Merleau-Ponty, has his composite Bressonian persona say: 'il y a comme une essence de la mort qui est toujours à l'horizon de mes pensées'[21] (Godard 1966: 59). Of no Bresson film is this truer than of *Mouchette*, his second Bernanos adaptation, shot in late 1966 and released the following year. Marvin Zeman's claim that Bresson was heading towards suicide finds more support in *Mouchette* that in any other of the director's works (Zeman 1971). A character named – or more accurately nicknamed – Mouchette figures in two Bernanos novels, *Sous le soleil de Satan* (1926) and *Nouvelle histoire de Mouchette* of eleven years later. Bresson's film is adapted from the later text; Maurice Pialat was to film *Sous le soleil de Satan* in 1987, with Sandrine Bonnaire and Gérard Depardieu whose very presence is sufficient indication of how far removed his film is from the Bressonian universe.

21 'there is something like an essence of death always on the horizon of my thoughts.'

Like *Journal*, *Mouchette* (produced by Anatole Dauman) is set in a spiritually and materially impoverished village community. The action of the novel is transposed from the Pas-de-Calais in Northern France, where Bernanos lived for many years, to Provence, but a Provence a world away from Peter Mayle or Claude Berri's Pagnol adaptations, prefiguring rather the harshly exploitative universe of Sandrine Veysset's *Y aura-t-il de la neige à Noël?* (*Will it snow for Christmas?*) (1996). There is no equivalent to the wealthy count and his family in *Journal*; most if not all of Mouchette's large family sleep in one room, when she has to warm the bottle for the baby's milk there are no more matches, and her drunken father seemingly gives her no pocket money (only a glass of gin in the village café). The poverty is grimmer and more universal than in any of Bresson's other work, one reason why the film is among his most pessimistic. René Gardies describes it as 'le seul film de Bresson véritablement sombre'[22] (Gardies 1967: 146). Bernanos was inspired to write his novel by seeing lorryloads of Spanish republicans being driven off to be shot during the Spanish Civil War. *Mouchette*, made when the Vietnam war was at its height, makes no reference to events outside its village, but is suffused with a despair about western 'civilisation' very much of its time. Like *Journal*, its texture is less sensual and baroque than the source novel, but in other ways the two films are strikingly different.

Nowhere is this plainer than in their contrasting attitudes towards language. The priest suffers appalling isolation, but through his diary is able to articulate, and if the final cross is to be believed, overcome it. Language in *Mouchette* is used with extreme sparseness, and frequently to lie or hurt rather than to communicate; Georges Sadoul describes it as 'en quelque sorte un film muet'[23] (Sadoul 1984: 123). The film's opening shot is of Mouchette's mother in church wondering aloud – presumably to an absent God – what will become of her family after her impending death, and the film's ending reveals her fears to be more than justified. Whether it is the teacher's humiliation of

22 'Bresson's only really sombre film.'
23 'in some sense a silent film.'

Mouchette because she cannot sing in tune, the shopkeeper's calling her a slut or her father slapping her angrily as she is about to speak to the young man who smiled at her on the dodgem-cars, the acts of communication in which she is involved are nearly all brutalising ones. Her naïvety and lack of psychological development (in both senses of the term) are intimately linked with this. In the *Cahiers* interview about *Balthazar*, Bresson spoke of his wish in *Mouchette* once again to concentrate on just one character, and to take 'la petite fille la plus maladroite, la moins actrice, la moins comédienne', in order to try to 'tirer d'elle tout ce qu'elle ne soupçonnera pas que je tire d'elle'[24] (Godard and Delahaye 1966: 71). This, in the light of the rape scene in Arsène's hut and Marie Cardinal's denunciation of how Bresson supposedly treated Nadine Nortier (Cardinal 1967), seems to lend disturbing weight to Oudart's thesis that Bresson in some sense films his own Sadean relationship with his actresses (or female *modèles*). Without first-hand knowledge of the filming or access to Mlle Nortier it is impossible for me to pronounce further on this. What is clear is that Mouchette undergoes a destiny rather than living a life, in which respect she is, along with Balthazar, the archetypal Bressonian *modèle*. Bresson said in a *Le Monde* interview about this film: 'S'il y a analyse et psychologie dans mes films, c'est avec des images et plutôt à la manière des peintres portraitistes'[25] (Baby 1967: 72). That statement is particularly true of the two films discssed in this chapter, for largely opposite reasons – *Balthazar* because of its breadth of focus, *Mouchette* because it concentrates on one character who has little choice but to react to what happens to her, at least until the end. This may well underlie the antipathy to the film shared by Jacques Rivette and François Truffaut, for the latter of whom it displays 'une espèce d'inconscience, un côté scandaleux'[26] (Truffaut and Latil-Le Dantec 1997: 87).

The texture of the film, however, is less monotonous and

---

24 'the clumsiest young girl, the one who is least an actress, [in order to try to] extract from her everything she does not suspect me of extracting from her.'

25 'If there is analysis and psychology in my films, it is done through images, in the manner of a portrait painter.'

26 'a kind of unawareness, a scandalous aspect.'

downbeat than my account hitherto may suggest, and that for four reasons. First, while the use of speech is minimal – non-existent in the opening and closing sequences – Bresson still retains much of the dialogue from Bernanos's novel, and this often has a strikingly oneiric quality to it, imbued with naïve poetry. Thus, Mouchette twice describes the storm from which she takes refuge as a 'cyclone' – a term at once childlike in its repetition of the term used by Arsène and adult in its implicit awareness that in the context in which he has used it it has a metaphorical significance, indicating 'her nascent awareness of the world of psychic disorder' (Reader 1998: 441). Second, the use of the Monteverdi Magnificat at the beginning and end – the last occurrence of non-diegetic music in Bresson – suggests, as we shall see, a trans-cendence of the body and of suffering that is less unequivocal than in *Journal*, echoing rather the ending of *Balthazar*. Third, the use of sound – the crackling of vegetation as poacher and gamekeeper spy on each other at the beginning, the church bell tolling for nobody to hear as Mouchette walks through the village at the end, the final splash as she tumbles off-screen into the water – is for me the most powerful in the director's work, along, as Lindley Hanlon suggests, with *Un condamné* (Hanlon 1986: 138). This is precisely because these noises have to carry so much of the burden that in a more conventional film would be borne by dialogue and/or music. (I have 'watched' the end of *Mouchette* with my eyes closed from the point at which she speaks the film's final words and found its impact barely less than with them open – a perfect example of Bresson's injunction to 'supprimer l'image' where it can be replaced by a sound.) Finally, the film is, as Sémolué points out (Sémolué 1993: 161), visually among Bresson's richest – containing more long-shots than any other apart from *Affaires publiques*, presenting a broader tableau of village life, from hunting and poaching to the fun of the fair, than the more restrictively shot *Balthazar*.

The film opens with Mouchette's mother (Marie Cardinal) wondering what will become of her family after her death. Following the credits (and the first occurrence of the Monteverdi Magnificat), the gamekeeper, Mathieu, is seen largely but not solely in close-up spying upon the poacher Arsène, and freeing a partridge he has trapped in one of his snares. References to hunting and poaching in French cinema – another example is the end of Resnais's *Mon oncle d'Amérique* – inevitably connote Renoir's *La Règle du jeu*, in which the professional rivalry between the gamekeeper Schumacher and the poacher Marceau spills over into the private sphere when Marceau pays fruitful attentions to Schumacher's wife Lisette. The next scene shows the café waitress Louisa telling Arsène to go away but come back later, whereupon Mathieu arrives in the bar – a clear indication that a similar triangular intrigue is going on in Bresson's film. The drinking in the bar, here and hereinafter, is of a joylessly soggy kind that teeters on the brink of self-parody. Gin – the harsh schnapps-like beverage of northern France rather than the delicately perfumed product of Messrs Gordon – is swilled as though purely for its anaesthetic effect, and nobody so much as orders a drink for themselves, let alone buys a round; Louisa fills the empty glasses up as automatically as they are then emptied.

Mouchette's father and brother are seen unloading contraband alcohol from a lorry, clearly destined for the café. They return home drunk and we see the father, in a horrifyingly regressive image, lying on his mattress 'playing' at driving a lorry, using his cap as the steering wheel and imitating the noise of the engine. Mouchette takes care of the family as best she can and sets off for school, where she is bullied by the teacher for not being able to sing in tune – ironically, the song is about Christopher Columbus and his hopes for a better world. After the cheerless bar and the brutalising school, the third pillar of village life makes a depressing appearance as Mouchette is pushed violently into the church by her father. We then see her washing up in the café, reimbursed by Louisa – a scene which leads Sitney to suggest that Louisa is the only remotely positive role-model available to Mouchette in the film, and that the young girl's subsequent acceptance of Arsène's violation may have to do with her 'identification and ... rivalry with Louisa' (Sitney 1998: 148). She hands the money straight to her father but is then given the price of a dodgem-ride by a woman – an unexplained gesture that makes possible the film's, and Mouchette's, one moment of true pleasure. She whirls round at the wheel of her car, gleefully colliding with others and smiling flirtatiously at a young man, in a scene with no equivalent in the novel, whose fleeting celebration of the joy of movement evokes the motorcycle ride in *Journal*. She is then viciously slapped by her father while Arsène, on the dodgems with Louisa in his Sunday best, is being sought for a showdown by Mathieu.

The fact that the same *modèle* plays Arsène here and Arnold in *Balthazar* may tempt us into too ready a conflation of the two characters – similar in many respects, both extremely important in their films, but nevertheless also in some ways different. Both characters drink to chronic excess, but this is more marked for Arnold, if only because his milieu is a less uniformly sodden one, than for Arsène. Arsène on the dodgems, moreover, has two status symbols generally denied Arnold – a smart outfit (suit, collar and tie) and a desirable female companion. Arnold's usual garb of an aged overcoat and nothing else, with the periodic addition of footwear, suggests a degree of social maladaptation verging on the pathological, echoed in the solitary frenzy of his drinking and his quasi-autistic absence of anything resembling a sexual life. Arsène's epileptic fit, frightening for both Mouchette and the audience as it is, might seem almost 'normal' by comparison.

Mouchette, in a ditch beside the road, is seen for the second time throwing mud at some of her classmates – the only kind of communication she appears to have with those of her own age apart from the two occasions on which a boy exposes himself to her. Those two shots, like an earlier one in which young girls swing upside down on a fence to reveal their underpants, suggest the disturbing use of and attitude towards pubescent sexuality that is to become most apparent in the scene in Arsène's hut. The thirty years since *Mouchette*'s making have of course seen a vastly increased awareness of sexual politics in general and child abuse in particular, yet already in 1967 the fence shot was perceived – albeit by a deeply hostile witness, Georges de Coultray in *Positif* – to be far from innocent ('Ces postérieurs non professionnels avaient été longuement disposés par la main du maître'[27] (de Coultray 1967: 52). We are back with Bresson's 'Sadean' relationship with his *modèles*, here taking a particularly voyeuristic form.

Mouchette is caught in a rainstorm in the woods near Arsène's shack. Arsène and Mathieu fight savagely, but finally drink gin from the same bottle – a curiously reconciliatory moment absent from the novel. Mouchette takes refuge in Arsène's shack, where he uses a burning stick to cauterise the bite Mathieu has inflicted upon him. The hissing of the hot wood on Arsène's stoical, gin-numbed flesh, like the squelching as the two men roll in the soaking mud and their harsh laughter as they drink together, imbue this scene with an animal quality that is to extend to Arsène's rape of Mouchette too. The shack is a space at the limit of the human and the animal, the civilised and the instinctiual – the 'encounter of two consciousnesses' that are not just those of the sexually predatory poacher and the terrified Mouchette, but those of the human which recognises the law, forensic or Lacanian, and of the instinctual, the *ça* or id which predominates in the fight sequence and its aftermath.

The human reasserts itself when Arsène lights a fire to dry Mouchette and finds the clog she had lost in the mud – acts of everyday decency scarcely worthy of mention in a film less brutal than this, seeming to make of him the friend and accomplice she lacks. She counters his fear that he may have dealt Mathieu a fatal injury (as much of an exaggeration as his use of the term 'cyclone', suggesting, like it, the delirium that is shortly to erupt) by saying: 'Je les déteste. Je leur tiendrai tête à tous'.[28] The blanket affirmation of 'les', the stubborn promise to stand up to 'tous', place Mouchette firmly within the symbolic space of the shack, outside the world of the village she here abjures and to which she is only briefly to return. If anywhere in the film (the bumper-car idyll apart) Mouchette can be said to have found a place for herself, it is here, in paradoxical solidarity with a fellow outcast.

The harmony, of however bizarre a kind, she seems to have

---

27 'Those non-professional posteriors had been lengthily set in place by the master's touch.'
28 'I hate them. I'll stand up to the lot of them.'

discovered is embodied in her comforting Arsène after his epileptic fit, when she is able to sing the 'Christophe Colomb' song in tune. It is violently shattered when she is raped. She flails her arms in a despairing attempt to beat off the assault, then stretches them out in a cross-like shape, and finally clasps them round Arsène. This *ne plus ultra* in Mouchette's acceptance of what is imposed on her is, as I have already suggested, deeply disturbing. Stefan Schädler's assertion that 'there are no more actors and sacrifices, but an understanding' (Buchka *et al.* 1978 [my translation]: 146) is hardly adequate to deal with it; even – especially – on a Christo-centric reading of the scene, that 'understanding' is relayed through, is dependent for its very existence upon, a sacrifice of a particularly horrific kind. The imagery of the Cross is important for an understanding not just of this scene, but of the whole film. Mouchette can in different ways be likened to each of the three figures present at the foot of the Cross at the end – Christ in her opening of her arms in sacrifice, Mary the virgin mother in her tending to her family and the 'fallen woman' Mary Magdalene when she proclaims to Mathieu's wife that Arsène is her lover. What disappears between these three – what is never available for her from the start – is any possibility of a 'normal' life in which sex and motherhood might be associated with happiness and choice. We know now, far more clearly than thirty years ago, that victims of sexual abuse can grow to become emotionally dependent upon – even to love – their abusers. Bresson presents us with a shock-ingly condensed view of that process, and in what follows with Mouchette's initial acceptance of, then final reaction against, it.

No longer a virgin, her maternal role becomes more oppressive when her mother dies, her father's most emotional reaction to his bereavement a snarl of: 'As-tu bientôt fini de me regarder comme ça, espèce de malapprise?' to which Mouchette replies: 'Merde'.[29] What follows is her final walk through the village, readable in hindsight as an unspoken farewell. Her first port of call is the woman shopkeeper who offers her coffee and croissants, and looks suspiciously at her open blouse; it is in response to the

---

29 'Will you stop looking at me like that, you ill-brought-up brat?' … 'Shit.'

sexual implications of this glance that Mouchette 'accidentally on purpose' breaks the bowl of coffee, as though in a final attempt at defending an innocence gone for ever. Next she is called over by Mathieu's wife, to whom she asserts that Arsène is her lover – ambiguously a clinging to solidarity with him, the verbal equivalent of her clasp in the shack, and/or a weary acceptance, doubtless bred in her through her childhood, of the grimly exploitative sexuality around her. Her final visit is to the elderly lady who gives her a winding-sheet for her mother and speaks of her love for the tranquillity of death – a rural grotesque like a mirror-image of the avariciously death-detesting miller in *Balthazar*. It is to her that Mouchette's final words – 'Vous me dégoûtez, sale vieille bête!'[31] – are spoken, indication surely of the angry rejection implicit in what follows.

She walks past a wood in which hares are being shot – a *La Règle du jeu*-like prefiguration of the human death to come – and lies down on a sloping bank beside a pond, wrapping around herself a white muslin dress given to her by the 'sale vieille bête'. She rolls down the bank and stops short at the water's edge; walking back up the slope she spies a tractor in whose direction she waves. The driver ignores her and passes on. 'Not waving but drowning', Mouchette walks back up the bank and through the crackling vegetation rolls down a second time. Once more she stops short and walks back up the slope, to fall for a third time – like Christ – into the water – like Burne-Jones's Ophelia except that she disappears off-screen. There is a loud splash – like Mouchette, we feel the weight of the body at this point – and Monteverdi's Magnificat is heard for the last time.

That Magnificat – the joyous submission of a virgin to the news of her motherhood – has an ironic appropriateness to Mouchette's situation, much as the Annunciation has in *Les Dames*. It is significant that Bresson chose a non-vocal passage from a vocal work (the Venetian Vespers) for this scene, for that figures the disappearance of the body, and perhaps also the freeing of the soul, that from the ending of *Journal* through to Jeanne d'Arc's burning has been one

---

30 'You sicken me, you dirty old creature!'

of the most important themes in his work. This is why the ending of *Mouchette* does not seem to me an unequivocally pessimistic one. We shall see that in his next film, *Une femme douce*, that theme occupies an even more important place.

References

Affron, Mirella Jona (1998) 'Bresson and Pascal: Rhetorical Affinities', in James Quandt (ed.), *Robert Bresson*, Toronto, Cinematheque Ontario.

Arnaud, Philippe (1986), *Robert Bresson*, Paris, Cahiers du Cinéma.

Baby, Y. (1967), 'Le Domaine de l'indicible', *Le Monde*, 14 March.

Benayoun, Robert (1966), 'Cannes vingt: olé!' *Positif*, no 79.

Browne, Nick (1977), 'Narrative point of view: the rhetoric of *Au hasard Balthazar*', *Film Quarterly*, vol. 31/1.

Buchka, Peter; Prinzler, Hans Helmut, Schädler, Stefan, and Vitte, Karsten (1978), *Robert Bresson*, Munich, Hansen.

Cardinal, Marie (1967), *Cet été-là*, Paris, Julliard.

de Coultray, Georges (1967), 'Une affaire de trahison', in *Positif*, no. 85.

Deleuze, Gilles (1983), *Cinéma 1: L'Image–mouvement*, Paris, Minuit.

Duras, Marguerite (1997), 'Au hasard Balthazar', in *Robert Bresson: Éloge*, Milan/ Paris,

France Soir, 17 May 1966.

Gardies, René (1967), '*Au hasard Balthazar*', *Image et son*, no. 207.

Godard, Jean-Luc (1966), 'Le Testament de Balthazar', *Cahiers du cinéma*, no. 177.

Godard, Jean-Luc, and Delahaye, Michel, (1966), 'La Question', *Cahiers du cinéma*, no. 178.

Hanlon, Lindley (1986), *Fragments: Bresson's Film Style*, Cranbury, London and Toronto, Associated University Presses.

Pascal, Blaise ([1670] 1976), *Pensées*, Paris, GF-Flammarion.

Reader, Keith (1998), '"D'où cela vient-il?": notes on three films by Robert Bresson', in James Quandt (ed.), *Robert Bresson*, Cinematheque Ontario, Toronto.

Robbe-Grillet, Alain (1984), *Pour un nouveau roman*, Paris, Minuit.

Sadoul, Georges (1984), *Rencontres I: chroniques et entretiens*, Paris, Denoël.

Sémolué, Jean (1993), *Bresson ou l'acte pur des métamorphoses*, Paris, Flammarion.

Sitney, P. Adams (1998), 'Cinematography vs. the Cinema: Bresson's Figures', in James Quandt (ed.), *Robert Bresson*, Cinematheque Ontario, Toronto.

Truffaut, François and Latil-Le Dantec, Mireille (1997), 'Entretien sur Robert Bresson', in *Robert Bresson: Hommage*, Milan and Paris, Mazzotta/Cinémathèque française.

Wollen, Peter (1970), *Signs and Meaning in the Cinema*, London, Thames & Hudson/BFI.

Zeman, Marvin (1971), 'The Suicide of Robert Bresson', *Cinema* (Beverly Hills), vol 6/3.

5

Bresson and Dostoevsky: *Une femme douce* and *Quatre nuits d'un rêveur*

Bresson's next two films, his first in colour, are also his first true adaptations from Dostoevsky. The short stories, or more accurately novellas, from which they are taken are from opposite ends of Dostoevsky's career: *A Gentle Creature*, adapted in 1969 as *Une femme douce*, was published in 1876, after the great novels and only four years before the end of Dostoevsky's life, while *White Nights*, on which *Quatre nuits d'un rêveur* (1972) is based, is from 1848. *White Nights* had also been filmed in 1957 by the Italian director Luchino Visconti, whose filmic style is very far removed from Bresson's.

The films' contiguity of date and inspiration makes them obvious companion pieces, as does the presence in each of them of a characteristically Bressonian *femme douce* – in the film of that title, indeed, *the* exemplar of the genre. So too does their use of colour. Bresson seems to me not to be a director whose work cries out for colour from the beginning, as might be said for example of Godard, nor, on the other hand, one like the Resnais of *L'Année dernière à Marienbad* making films that would be inconceivable other than in black and white. (If I find it more difficult to imagine a colour version of *Journal* than of any of the other films, this is doubtless because of the persistent gloom of the mood and setting, which makes the film a prolonged study in grey and black.) Bresson's own remarks on the cinema have shown no interest in colour *per se*, leaving a strong impression that when it became available he was perfectly willing to use it without according it major importance. Close-ups tend to be rarer in his colour than in his monochrome films; indeed, 'the only extreme close-up of a person' (Hanlon 1986: 45) in *Une femme douce* is of the heroine immediately before she leaps to her death. A reason for this is suggested by Fredric Jameson's paradoxical observation that '[c]olor ... spells the end of filmic and photographic realism *and* modernism alike' – this, because its naturalism (in the sense in which Lukàcs opposes the term to realism) diverts attention from 'the strangeness of representationality itself'. Jameson's view of 'the black-and-white glossy print as an object in the world, both *like* this last and distinct and stylised from it' (Jameson 1992: 192) could scarcely be bettered as a description of the great Bresson monochrome films, and may suggest why for me at any rate they continue to represent, along with *L'Argent*, the peak of his work.

The reservations about Bresson's colour work implicit in that last sentence are especially marked for the two films discussed in this chapter. *Quatre nuits d'un rêveur* in particular (hereinafter *Quatre nuits*) seems to me closer to self-parody in the mannered-ness of its acting than any other of Bresson's works, and that problem is compounded by the fact that neither film is readily available on video. I had seen both – *Une femme douce* several times, *Quatre nuits* only once – on 16 mm many years before embarking on this book, and was able to refresh my memory with screenings arranged by the Paris Cinémathèque. Inevitably, however, I feel less sure of my ground here than anywhere else in the *œuvre* – a reason, but not an excuse, for any crying weaknesses in this chapter.

Une femme douce

Bresson said in an interview with *Cinema Canada* in January 1969: 'I believe that once a couple understand each other they can no longer stand each other' (Rhode 1970: 82). The ending of *Pickpocket* might suggest otherwise, but that of *Une femme douce* is all too congruent with the grimness of that view. Jonas Mekas describes the film as being about diagonals (Mekas 1997: 52), structuring the obliquity of a relationship without real communication. It is Bresson's first film to begin – like the novella from which it is taken – with a flashback, to the suicide of the wife which the despairing husband spends the rest of the film reconstructing and trying in a further series of flashbacks to understand. The flashback can often work, as classically in Carné's *Le Jour se lève*, to produce a sense of the inevitability of destiny, and that is clearly its effect here.

Une femme douce's destiny of incomprehension is, as its title reminds us, a strongly gendered one. In this respect it evokes films as different as Truffaut's *Jules et Jim* and Nicholas Roeg's *Bad Timing*, in which the central female character refuses to be understood by one or more probing males. The ending, of novella and film alike, seals that destiny – Dostoevsky's widowed husband self-pityingly asking 'when they take her away tomorrow, what on earth am I going to do?' (Dostoevsky [1846] 1995: 103), Bresson's watching in despair as the lid is screwed down on the coffin. As Jean-Pierre Oudart points out, this is Bresson's first film not only to end but to begin with a death, which thus constitutes a 'dédoublement temporel de la fiction'.[1] That doubling-up is also one of gender, constructed for Oudart along Lacanian lines by the identification of the male with desire and the female with demand. This somewhat essentialist formulation nevertheless works well for an (oxymoronic?) understanding of *Une femme douce*. 'Ce qui fait problème ici, pour Bresson, c'est le rapport entre un désir (celui du moi) qui s'inscrit dans l'écart de la différence absolue (la femme absolument autre, opaque, silencieuse) qui le suscite, et une demande (qui est d'abord celle de la femme)'[2] (Oudart 1969: 55). The husband's repeated desire for his wife's body – verging in the voice-over on the necrophiliac – and her never satisfied demand for his love are constant throughout the film. It is the 'absolute

---

1 'a temporal doubling-up of the fiction.'
2 'What poses a problem here, for Bresson, is the relationship between a desire (that of the ego) inscribed in the gap of the absolute difference (the woman as absolutely other, opaque, silent) that arouses it, and a demand, in the first instance that of the woman.'

difference' between them that in the end literally precipitates her suicide. Desire and demand, for Lacan, are associated with the metonymic and the metaphorical respectively, which is to say that the first is closer to structuralist and post-structuralist notions of language as a signifying chain of difference and the second to earlier, less 'sophisticated' views of it as grounded in identity and referentiality. The desiring male desires difference, including – especially – his wife's; the demanding female demands a unitary loving presence, reminiscent of that of the father (in the novella she is an orphan). The husband's bitter regrets, in both texts, about the silence that rapidly became a habit between them find an explanation here. That silence distilled a linguistic incompatibility that was also a profoundly gendered one.

The lead roles in *Une femme douce* are taken by Dominique Sanda (shortly afterwards to star in Bertolucci's *The Conformist*) and Guy Frangin, a painter Bresson had met at an exhibition. The *nouveau romancier* Claude Ollier appears in the minor role of the doctor. If *Balthazar* and *Mouchette* had marked Bresson's engagement with the modernisation of rural France, *Une femme douce* does likewise for Paris, which is to be the increasingly pessimistic locale for all his remaining films except *Lancelot du lac*. Places of entertainment and culture play a prominent part in the film, but almost always in ways that undercut their ostensible function. The intellectual epicentre of Paris, Saint-Germain-des-Prés, makes its first appearance in Bresson, but it is as the setting for a jealous pursuit. The Venuses and Psyches the couple see in the Louvre arouse admiration in the wife, but make the husband see woman as an instrument of pleasure – a confusion of representation and represented too elementary not to be ironic. Their film and theatre outings, meticulously budgeted for by the husband, are little more successful. The film they go to see – Michel Deville's *Benjamin ou les mémoires d'un puceau* (*Benjamin or the memoirs of a male virgin*) – is a mannered eighteenth-century costume piece during the screening of which a young man in the audience makes advances to the wife. They also go to an overblown and overacted performance of *Hamlet*, an episode seen by Hanlon as catalysing the wife's decision to take her life (Hanlon 1986: 54–7). Both film and play are at the antipodes of Bresson's own ideas on acting – a point reinforced when the couple return home after *Hamlet* and the wife reads out from her own edition of Shakespeare a passage omitted in the performance ('Speak the speech, I pray you, as I pronounced it to you, trippingly on the tongue. But if you mouth it, as many of our players do, I had as lief the town crier spoke my lines').[3] What is denounced here is not merely an acting style (though that is clearly part of it), but the self-centred hollowness of the husband's emotional rhetoric – inevitably more perceptible in Dostoevsky than in Bresson.

Despite the film's dearth of close-ups and comparative breadth of topographical reference, it is still characteristically Bressonian in being a very claustrophobic work. The arid neatness of the couple's flat, which the wife disrupts with loud music, makes it something like a prison, an impression which is intensified by her financial dependence on the husband and his business. The determinedly non-reverberant voices in which the couple speak also contribute to the claustrophobic atmosphere. Danièle Heyman in *L'Express* (14 September 1969) compared their voices to that of the computer Hal in Kubrick's *2001: A Space Odyssey*; a more sympathetically analytical view comes from Serge Cardinal for whom they speak 'comme si la voix toute entière était une introjection sonore. Face à l'activité de l'appareil vocal se dresse l'abstraction de la voix'[4] (Cardinal 1995: 7). Introjection, for Freud and after him Melanie Klein, is a way for the child to deal with that which it perceives as threatening by absorbing it. The husband and wife (it scarcely seems appropriate to speak of them as a 'couple' in this context) clutch their utterances to themselves, so that even their most intimate communication is contaminated by silence – not the speaking silence of psychoanalysis, but the simpler and more deadly silence of the grave.

Une femme douce opens with a medium shot of an empty rocking-chair on a balcony, followed by a longer shot of a white shawl fluttering through the air (cf. Mouchette's winding-sheet).

---

3 Shakespeare's *Hamlet*, III (ii).
4 'as if the whole voice were an introjection of sound. In opposition to the activity of the vocal apparatus is to be found the abstraction of the voice.'

The young woman is then shown lying lifeless on the pavement, already dead on our first sight of her. Cut to her body lying on a bed in the couple's flat, flanked by the husband and the elderly housekeeper Anna whose hands are shown joined in prayer; her head, in a Dreyeresque evocation of the transcendental impersonality of the gesture, remains invisible. The husband calls to mind how his wife seemed barely sixteen on their first meeting, in Oudart's perspective doubtless a *mise en abyme* (like the entire film?) of Bresson's perverse relationship with his female *modèles*. Flashback to the antique shop in which the husband is shown treating the clients very brusquely. In the Dostoevsky novella he is a wrongly discharged army officer who has resentfully been obliged to take up pawnbroking; Bresson's milieu, characteristically, is more comfortably bourgeois, and nothing is said of how the film's husband came to exercise his profession. The *femme douce* brings him a series of objects, initially of derisory worth but becoming more valuable, until she comes in with a small crucifix. In an all too comprehensible gesture, he buys the gold setting and discards the ivory Christ. These episodes, like many others in this film, can be seen as equivalent to the imperfect tense, representing what regularly happened or typically used to happen during the couple's relationship. Orson Welles famously used such episodes in *Citizen Kane* to show the decay of Kane's relationship with Susan through a series of breakfast-table scenes, cited by Christian Metz as a prime example of what he calls the 'séquence par épisodes'/'episodic sequence' (Metz 1968: 132). Welles is about as far removed from Bresson as any film-maker could be, and indeed never made any secret of his lack of regard for Bresson's work, so that I should be loath to press this comparison too far. Yet the strangeness of *Une femme douce* may be rendered somewhat less forbidding, though thereby also less Bressonian, through at least a partial comparison with a classic cinematic narrative technique.

The husband quotes Mephistopheles's description of himself in Goethe's *Faust* (where he speaks of being a part of that force which sometimes wishes evil, sometimes does good) – a force we have often enough seen at work in Bresson, notably in *Pickpocket*, but one we may here suspect the director of invoking with a touch of irony. The husband's deployment of his high culture is what the French would call 'BCBG' – *bon chic bon genre*, impeccably 'dinner party' as might be said in a British context. This implies that it is also, as the disastrous theatre and cinema outings mentioned earlier suggest, soulless and artificial, in contrast to the spontaneity with which the wife plays Purcell or rock music as the fancy takes her. Like Rohmer, a film-maker with whom he has little else in common, Bresson in his later films especially takes his characters' cultural pretensions less seriously than hostile critics may allow.

Their first joint expedition is to the zoo – reminiscent of *Balthazar* and of Chabrol's *Les Bonnes Femmes*, in which the shopgirls of the title pay it a visit. A later trip will be to the natural history museum in the Jardin des Plantes, evoking 'man's common bond with all living creatures' (Hanlon 1986: 52), but perhaps more ironically than Hanlon's solemn references to Claudel and Teilhard de Chardin may suggest. What humanity by definition shares with the other animals, after all, is instinct, and prominent among our instincts is that of flight from a situation judged dangerous or intolerable – an instinct with which the film has opened and on which we know it must also close.

There is an unmistakably celebratory quality about the couple's lovemaking when they return to their flat after the wedding – the first scene in Bresson to show, or at least hint at, sexual fulfilment. Yet the husband, whose status as what would nowadays be called a 'control freak' is surely no longer in doubt, tells us in voice-over that he sought to 'jeter de l'eau froide sur cet enivrement',[5] by expounding his views on how best the couple might amass money – a truly classic Freudian move. His subsequent remorseful voice-over ('Oh! pourquoi, dès le début, avons-nous adopté le silence?')[6] acquires great ironic force from being addressed to Anna – 'the viewer's surrogate in the fiction' (Hanlon 1986: 34), through her role as mutely observing witness. The words the couple might have exchanged, like their caresses, are displaced and transmuted

5 'to throw cold water on this intoxication.'
6 'Oh! why from the beginning were we silent with each other?'

into the currency, literal and metaphorical, of a sterile albeit cultured existence.

Quarrels begin over the wife's habit of paying clients more than their objects are worth, miserliness here as often acting for Bresson as an index of spiritual impoverishment. She returns late one evening and will not say where she has been – an episode that we may reconstruct retrospectively as part of the relationship (of whatever kind) with the mysterious man with whom she is later found in his car. The husband's response to her refusal ('Je ne peux pas ne pas savoir')[7] resembles an assertion of proprietorial rights. The double negative also brings it close to the jealousy that at once sustains and destroys the love of Swann for Odette in Proust, a favourite author of Bresson's. Swann's 'jalousie, comme une pieuvre qui jette une première, puis une seconde, puis une troisième amarre, s'attacha solidement à ce moment ... puis à un autre, puis à un autre encore'[8] (Proust [1913/19] 1954: 283). This metonymic 'feeding frenzy' is not developed in *Une femme douce*, which is not an anatomy of jealousy; but those who know Proust will be reminded of it by the sequence where the husband tours Saint-Germain-des-Prés in pursuit of his wife much as Swann seeks Odette in every restaurant along the boulevards. Dostoevsky's husband spies on his wife as she rebuffs the advances of her admirer, an encounter he describes as 'a duel between a woman of the most exalted nobility and a worldly, dull-witted creature with the soul of a reptile' (Dostoevsky [1846] 1995: 80). The irony, of course, is that that description could equally well apply to the course of the marriage thenceforth, in book and film alike. Bresson shows us wife and admirer together in a car near the Boulevard Lannes, which in an evocation of *Les Dames* runs alongside the Bois de Boulogne in the sixteenth *arrondissement* – an exclusive residential area, but also close to a park renowned for prostitution and illicit sexual encounters. He drags her away, not before reassuring himself on the basis of what he has heard that

7 'I cannot not know.'
8 '[his] jealousy, like an octopus putting down first one, then a second, then a third mooring, fastened firmly on to this moment, then on to another, then on to one more.'

his wife is innocent of any carnal involvement. That night they spend apart, and the following morning she places his revolver against his head; he feigns sleep. We may be reminded here of Mauriac's *Thérèse Desqueyroux*, in which the heroine attempts to poison her husband in a gesture of protest against the sterile claustrophobia of their marriage. The wife falls ill for six weeks, after which the husband takes her to more places of culture and entertainment, reassuring himself and the still mute Anna that he took care of her 'comme un vrai mari'.[9] Yet, even if we did not already know of the tragedy in store, the animal skeletons they see at the museum would act as an ironic index of what their relationship has become.

They plan a journey together – the classic 'second honeymoon', save only that they have not had a first – and the wife promises: 'Je serai pour vous une femme fidèle. Je vous respecterai'.[10] His impassioned embrace of her after those words is yet another irony of incomprehension in this film so full of them, following incongruously on her affirmation of duty; is it the wife he desires or her fidelity and respect, her 'wifeliness?' Her suicide shortly afterwards, in this light, may well be catalysed by that embrace, standing as it does for a whole narrative of imposition and possession, and her final brief conversation with Anna ('Êtes-vous heureuse? – Oui, heureuse')[11] is tragically ironic in the full sense of that term. That happiness is distilled in the serenity of the close-up – as mentioned earlier, unique in the film – which immediately precedes her final leap, fulfilling an analogous role to the Monteverdi Magnificat in *Mouchette*. The wretched (in both senses) husband, left behind as the film returns to its framing narrative, can only plead for her to open her eyes, closed for ever now as his have in a sense been throughout the film.

The seeming unmotivatedness of the wife's suicide is thus paradoxically also what saves it from the 'purely' tragic. Of her, as of Mouchette, it can be said that 'on ne peut pas la réduire à ses actes, qui la trahissent au moins autant qu'ils l'expriment:

9 'like a real husband.'
10 'I'll be a faithful wife for you. I shall respect you.'
11 'Are you happy? – Yes, happy.'

l'essentiel est ailleurs'.[12] Between suicide and *mauvaise foi*, there is perhaps a bitter consolation to be derived from the choice of the former.

Quatre nuits d'un rêveur

Quatre nuits d'un rêveur, largely but I suspect not solely because it has been unviewable for so long, is probably the least written-about of Bresson's films; it did poorly at the box office, and Carlos Clarens's prediction that it was 'headed for a low place in the director's canon' (Clarens 1971–72: 3) has on the whole been fulfilled. Its central character (Jacques), closely modelled on the unnamed hero of *White Nights*, also belongs to a type familiar to us from New Wave and post-New Wave cinema – the existentially disaffected young man with vague pretensions to creativity, often incarnated by Jean-Pierre Léaud. That I should do something so unBressonian as invoke an actor – the New Wave actor *par excellence* – in discussing this film may indicate how atypical of the director's work in many ways it is. Incomparably more manic though the Léaud persona is, its affinities with Jacques, played by Guillaume des Forêts (son of the poet Louis-René), are manifest. The narcissistic loop in which Jacques is caught as he listens to the tape-recording of himself repeating Marthe's name is reminiscent of Léaud/Antoine Doinel in Truffaut's *Baisers volés* (1968), watching himself in the mirror as he obsessively chants the name of his love-object, Fabienne Tabard. (Jean Sémolué has remarked on the similarities between the Truffaut film and *Quatre nuits* – Sémolué 1993: 189.)

We may think too of Léaud avatars subsequent to *Quatre nuits* – Tom in Bertolucci's *Last Tango in Paris* of 1972 and Alexandre in Jean Eustache's *La Maman et la putain* from the following year. Tom films as manically as Jacques tape-records himself, while *Quatre nuits*'s boat named *Marthe* after Bresson's heroine finds an echo in a boat in the Bertolucci film named *L'Atalante*. This

12 'she cannot be reduced to her acts, which betray her as much as they express her. The essential is elsewhere.'

parallel is reinforced by a shot in *Quatre nuits* of a *bateau-mouche* from a similar angle to the canal boat at the end of Vigo's *L'Atalante*. Alexandre's dogged pursuit of women in *La Maman et la putain* echoes Jacques's in its ultimately castratory futility, and the role of Gilberte in the Eustache film is taken by Isabelle Weingarten (daughter of the playwright Romain) who here plays Marthe. There is even a sartorial echo in the shawl constantly worn by Véronika in *La Maman et la putain*, similar to Marthe's in the Bresson film – a minor but telling illustration of how so idiosyncratic and seemingly ahistorical a film-maker can, nowhere more than in *Quatre nuits*, find his work bearing the imprint of the *Zeitgeist*. The hippy characters and music that infelicitously bestrew the film are the clearest example of this.

Quatre nuits is generally regarded as being lighter in tone than any of Bresson's other work (always excepting *Affaires publiques*), because of its curiously ambiguous 'happy ending' and the fact that it begins with a suicide averted rather than closing on one committed like its two predecessors. It is hardly surprising that at about this time Marvin Zeman predicted, as it turned out erroneously, that Bresson himself was heading for suicide (Zeman 1971). The nearest bridges to Bresson's Paris home are the Pont Louis-Philippe and the Pont Saint-Louis, neither of which has the multiple resonances of the Pont Neuf. Despite its name this is Paris's oldest bridge, which inspired the expression 'Vous vous portez comme le Pont Neuf',[13] famously addressed at the end of Proust's *Le Côté de Guermantes* by the Duc de Guermantes to the dying Swann (Proust [1913/19] 1954: 597). More recently, it was the décor for Léos Carax's *Les Amants du Pont Neuf* (1991) – a radically unBressonian film, but one whose emotionally and physically ravaged central characters could almost be the damaged descendants of Bresson's hippies and drifters.

One critic who does not share the general view of *Quatre nuits* as the lightest of the mature Bresson works is, perhaps unsurprisingly, Jean-Pierre Oudart. For Oudart, Jacques is not the likeable clown he may appear in the film's opening shots (hitch-

---

13 'You're in great shape.'

hiking towards Normandy, rolling around in a field, hitching back to Paris), but rather so utterly economically and sexually shut out of 'his' narrative as to be 'donné comme psychotique'[14] (Oudart 1972: 88). The static filming of the episodes in his room, contrasting with the much more mobile shooting of the outdoor scenes (Prédal 1992: 101), does indeed work to immobilise Jacques, whose foreclosure according to Oudart makes him a surrogate for and representative of Bresson's 'travail de dénégation'. The maxim of that work is supposedly to 'ne jamais inscrire le sexuel et l'économique selon l'ordre des désirs du sujet Bresson pour les minettes bourgeoises (ou travesties en prolétaires), ni selon ses intérêts pour l'argent'[15] (Oudart 1972: 87). Yet Jacques's radical outsideness, which Oudart's remarks stress, is scarcely any more marked than that of Michel in *Pickpocket*. In one sense, indeed, it can be seen as less so, for Michel's radical estrangement, suggested by his never-varying dress and the caricatural bleakness of his room, verges on the atemporal, whereas, as I have suggested, Jacques is much more a child of his time. Michel Estève draws attention to the importance for both Dostoevsky and Visconti of the 'thématique de l'amour-sentiment', figured in *Quatre nuits* through Jacques but less important there because Marthe's desire for the unnamed tenant introduces 'la notion moderne de sexualité comme origine et lieu de la passion' (Estève 1983: 71).[16] This suggests that the overtly sexual quality of this film compared to the earlier Bresson probably has more to do with the France of its time than with the bad faith Oudart seems to impute to 'le sujet Bresson'.

The film is clearly structured in six 'chapters' – four recounting the four nights of the title, the other two flashbacks to the 'histoire de Jacques' and 'histoire de Marthe' intercalated into the second night. The 'histoire de Marthe' corresponds to 'Nastenka's Story'

14 'represented as psychotic.'
15 'This work of denial' 'never inscribes the sexual and the economic within the desires of the subject Bresson for middle-class dolly-birds (even if they are disguised as proletarian), or his interest in money.'
16 'the theme of emotional love' 'the modern notion of sexuality as the origin and site of passion.'

in the Dostoevsky, except that in the book Nastenka (like the *femme douce*) is an orphan living with her grandmother. The 'histoire de Jacques' has no direct counterpart; what we learn about Jacques there is suggested by the first-person Dostoevskyan narrative. After the opening hitch-hiking shots described above, we see Jacques on the Pont Neuf, where he notices Marthe taking off her shoes and climbing over the parapet. He helps her onto the bridge and takes her back to her home, telling her that he will be by the statue of Henri IV at one end of the bridge the following evening. There they both duly are, Marthe taking the initiative by asking Jacques to tell his story. If in *Une femme douce* the woman represented demand and the man desire, *Quatre nuits* in one way at least reverses that polarity. Marthe's curiosity – about Jacques here, in a more specifically erotic way about the tenant later – is an allotrope of her desire, while the single-mindedness of Jacques's obsession, in the end its own satisfaction, is surely closer to the order of demand.

Jacques gives his address, whereupon the voice-over commentary stops. We see him vaguely following young women in the street, but never (unlike his descendant Alexandre in *La Maman et la putain*) going so far as to approach them, for as he tells Marthe he has been countless times in love 'de personne, d'un idéal'.[17] There follows a return to the 'histoire de Jacques'[18] by way of a Metzian 'episodic sequence', showing Jacques following an elegant couple in the street, dictating into his tape-recorder a short novel presumably inspired by them, and tinkering with some paintings in progress before listening to the text he has recorded. Solitude, indecision and dilettantism, the sequence tells us, are the stuff of Jacques's everyday life. The arrival in his room of an old classmate from the Beaux-Arts art school reinforces rather than diminishes the impression of solitude, for Jacques initially does not recognise him. Nor is what transpires between them exactly a dialogue; the friend delivers himself of a portentous monologue on 'conceptual and adult painting' and takes his leave.

---

17 'with nobody, with an ideal.'
18 Sémolué, 1993 (184–8) provides a clear breakdown into narrative units to which I am much indebted.

The episode has obvious echoes of the two painters who ride upon Balthazar and his companion, though its irony is considerably less subtle.

We then return to Jacques and Marthe, or more precisely to Marthe telling Jacques her story. This focuses on her passion for her mother's new tenant, a figure described by Prédal as 'tout à fait improbable'[19] (Prédal 1992: 101). This implausibility resides primarily in Marthe's falling in love with, or at least conceiving a violent desire for, him without ever having seen his face. She catches a back view of him on his way into his room, and is then seen leafing through books he has lent her mother. In the Dostoevsky these are classics of literature (Walter Scott and Pushkin), which allays the grandmother's suspicions that he may have '"slipped some love-note in there"' (Dostoevsky [1846] 1995: 31); he does not of course need to do so, for the texts he sends have power of enchantment enough. Bresson replaces classic literature *tout court* by classics of erotic literature (such as John Cleland's *Fanny Hill*) – of a piece with his modernisation of the novella, but by the same token very dated for the contemporary viewer.

The next contact between Marthe and the tenant occurs when he blocks the lift she is in and asks her to go to the cinema with him. This is compared by Sémolué to the sequence in *Les Dames* where Hélène rushes down the stairs to head off Jean, who has just made his escape in the lift. The tenant is thus 'un meneur de jeu comme Hélène', much as his later tapping on the wall of Marthe's room makes of him 'un Fontaine expéditif' (Sémolué 1993: 193).[20] The flaw in this latter comparison in particular is that Fontaine is seeking freedom, while the tenant is engaging in behaviour that would nowadays be regarded as harassment. If Bresson's domineering relationship with his female *modèles* has a surrogate anywhere in this film, it is surely here – a projective identification reinforced by the film première for which the tenant provides Marthe and her mother with tickets. The film (which unlike its counterpart in *Une femme douce* was specially shot for inclusion here) is a laughably overstated gangster melodrama, the

19 'utterly implausible.'
20 'takes the initiative like Hélène' ... 'a fast-working version of Fontaine.'

very opposite of Bressonian cinematography. Marthe explains that the tenant later admitted to her that he had given them tickets for a bad film as a deliberate act of revenge after she had refused his invitation. What in *Une femme douce* acts as an index, ambiguously aesthetic and spiritual, of the husband's shortcomings here acquires a more aggressive – not to say sadistic – quality.

Prédal sees the tenant's role as that of 'la part du rêve face à laquelle le couple plus en creux de Marthe et de Jacques se définit' (Prédal 1992: 101).[21] His virtual invisibility can be understood in this light as that of a blank space for Marthe's fantasy of love, or indeed for Jacques's of himself as a more active, less Wertherian figure. Marthe is seen contemplating herself naked in the mirror (Bresson's first nude scene); the tenant knocks on the wall and she tiptoes to his door to look through the keyhole. This scene may appear to counter the traditional view of voyeurism as a male and/ or sadistic activity, but 'appear to' is surely the *mot juste*, for we see Marthe's nakedness, not what she sees. The curiosity these shots (might) satisfy is thus a conventionally heterosexual-male one. Marthe learns from her mother that the tenant is to leave, and goes to his room demanding that he take her with him. They make love while the mother vainly looks for Marthe, repeatedly calling her name in an echo of Marie's father wandering through the fields in *Balthazar*.

On the Pont Neuf, the tenant promises that he will meet Marthe in precisely a year, and sets off to the airport in a taxi to go to study in America. A year has gone by and we are back with Marthe and Jacques, understanding now the reason for Marthe's attempt at suicide. Jacques devises a letter for Marthe to send via mutual friends to the tenant, which as in the novella corresponds exactly to what she had been thinking, and agrees to act as 'postman' for her. It is on the bus taking him to deliver the letter that Jacques over and over again plays the tape-recording of his voice reciting Marthe's name, the sound as so often in Bresson contributing more than the image to perhaps the film's most memorable scene. Sémolué (Sémolué 1993: 97) likens the

21 'the dream-like aspect in relation to which the more passive couple of Marthe and Jacques is defined.'

repeated use of the tape-recorder to one of Jacques Tati's running gags, though Tati's work lacks the narcissism so pervasive in this film. The comparison earlier made with Léaud/Doinel in *Baisers volés* is also striking, but the two scenes are in one crucial respect very different. Doinel chants first Fabienne Tabard's name, then his own, in a rhythm of accelerating excitement that can only be described as onanistic, while Jacques's utter sexual foreclosure is figured in the absence of his own name and the dreamy languor with which he repeats 'Marthe ... Marthe'. That Doinel, however briefly, becomes Fabienne's lover and Jacques does not become Marthe's accords with the different rhythms of their passions.

On the third night he again meets Marthe, who thanks him for not falling in love with her. Boats come and go, Latin American music drifts up from one of them, the tenant still does not appear, Jacques tries to explain away his absence and is rewarded by Marthe's telling him: 'Nous sommes liés pour toujours'.[22] The following morning Marthe is more of an obsession than ever; not only does he listen to her tape-recorded name as soon as he wakes, but he sees her name on a shop-front and, as already mentioned, on a barge. On the fourth night he admits his love to her (the first *tutoiement*, or use of the intimate form of address between them), and she in turn admits that he is worthier of her love than the absentee, who may only have been a way of emancipating herself from her mother. His response to this is to stroke her knee, as Jérôme/Jean-Claude Brialy does that of the eponymous heroine in Rohmer's *Le Genou de Claire* of the previous year. Jérôme's caress acts as summation of his desire for the (much younger) Claire, which thereafter will neither need nor want to go further, and the echo of his gesture in *Quatre nuits* is thus all too appropriate.

Jacques buys Marthe a scarf in the Saint-Germain-des-Prés drugstore, haunt of the trendy Parisian youth of the time, and she suggests that he rent a room in her mother's house. In an archetypally romantic gesture, he points out to her the moon in the sky ('être dans la lune', we may recall, is a French expression corresponding to 'having one's head in the clouds'). At that very

22 'We are joined for ever.'

moment she descries in the crowd the tenant, who asks if she is indeed Marthe. She runs to him, turns back to Jacques and kisses him on the cheeks, and walks off with the tenant – true love triumphant, some may think self-parodyingly so. The final scene shows Jacques back in his room/studio, recording a monologue in which art clearly compensates for the failings of life ('Elle me voit de loin. Elle vole à ma rencontre ... Oh, Marthe! Quelle force fait briller tes yeux d'une telle flamme, illumine ta figure d'un sourire pareil? Merci de ton amour. Et sois bénie pour le bonheur que tu m'apportes').[23] This evokes both the Dostoevsky text, which concludes even more ironically with: 'A whole moment of bliss! Is that not sufficient even for a man's entire life?' (Dostoevsky [1846] 1995: 56), and Michel's voice-over at the end of *Pickpocket*, referring as it does to the light that came over Jeanne's face. The narcissism of Jacques's listening to himself is replicated in his picking up his paintbrush, whose sound, moving across the canvas, closes the film in which 'Bresson s'ouvre pour la première fois au monde contemporain'. We may agree with Claire Clouzot that this is a 'curieuse tentative pour un homme aussi peu dans le siècle que lui'[24] (Clouzot 1972: 125).

This ending, ironic though it is, is nevertheless among the least pessimistic in Bresson – less so assuredly than that of *Une femme douce*. Marthe and the tenant are, we suppose, happy together (for how long it hardly seems pertinent to ask, any more than for Michel and Jeanne at the end of *Pickpocket*), and Jacques happy alone, with his solipsistic illusions and his art. None of the three films that were to succeed *Quatre nuits*, we shall see, was to allow even so tentative a measure of optimism.

---

23 'She sees me from afar. She rushes towards me ... Oh, Marthe! What force gives your eyes such a glow, illuminates your face with such a smile? Thank you for your love. And be blessed for the happiness you bring me.'
24 'Bresson opens himself for the first time to the contemporary world' ... 'a curious thing for a man so little of his time.'

References

Cardinal, Serge (1995), 'Le Lieu du son, l'espace de la voix. Autour d'*Une femme douce*', *Canadian Journal of Film Studies*, 4(2).

Clarens, Carlos (1971), '*Four Nights of a Dreamer*', *Sight and Sound*, winter 1971–72.

Clouzot, Claire (1972), *Le Cinéma français depuis la Nouvelle Vague*, Paris, Nathan.

Dostoevsky, Fyodor ([1846] 1995), *A Gentle Creature and other stories*, Oxford, Oxford University Press.

Estève, Michel (1983), *Robert Bresson: la passion du cinématographe*, Paris, Albatros.

Hanlon, Lindley (1986), *Fragments: Bresson's Film Style*, Cranbury, London and Toronto, Associated University Presses.

Jameson, Fredric (1992), *Signatures of the Visible*, London and New York, Routledge.

Mekas, Jonas (1997), 'Une femme douce', in *Robert Bresson: Éloge*, Milan and Paris, Mazzotta/Cinémathèque française.

Metz, Christian (1968), *Essais sur la signification au cinéma*, vol. 1, Paris, Klinksieck.

Oudart, Jean-Pierre (1969), 'La Suture', *Cahiers du cinéma*, no. 211.

Oudart, Jean-Pierre (1972), 'Le Hors-champ de l'auteur', *Cahiers du cinéma*, nos. 236–7.

Prédal, René (1992), *Robert Bresson: l'aventure intérieure, L'Avant-scène cinéma*, nos. 408–9.

Proust, Marcel ([1913/19] 1954), *A la recherche du temps perdu*, vols I and II, Paris, Pléiade.

Rhode, Eric (1970), 'Dostoevsky and Bresson', *Sight and Sound*, 39(2).

Sémolué, Jean (1993), *Bresson ou l'acte pur des métamorphoses*, Paris, Flammarion.

Zeman, Marvin (1971), 'The Suicide of Robert Bresson', *Cinema* (Beverly Hills), 6(3).

6

Sixth time lucky: *Lancelot du lac*

Bresson had originally intended to shoot *Lancelot du lac* (hereinafter *Lancelot*) immediately after *Journal*. It was then to be his next work over a period of fifteen years, the projected successor to each film up to and including *Balthazar*. Expense was the primary reason for each postponement, understandably so; the battle scenes in Rivette's *Jeanne la pucelle* were to show many years later how infelicitous the results of shooting would-be epic medieval footage on a shoestring budget could be. *Lancelot* was eventually made with finance from, among others, the state-owned broadcasting company ORTF, the actor–director Jean Yanne and the maverick producer Jean-Pierre Rassam. It has to be said that the film we know today would be inconceivable in monochrome; the use of red, by turns sombre and sanguinary, makes it the most striking and distinctive of Bresson's works in colour. The film enjoyed – especially after the modest reception of *Quatre nuits* – substantial success, being offered the International Critics' Prize at Cannes in 1974. Bresson refused this with the remark: 'Je ne veux pas du prestige, je veux de l'argent et seul la Palme d'Or attire de l'argent'[1] (*Combat* 28 May 1974) – some might think a churlish remark, but in the light of the funding difficulties that had been so much part of his career perhaps also an understandable one.

The 1996 issue of *Positif* largely devoted to Bresson contains details of an extraordinary correspondence between Bresson and

---

1 'I don't want prestige, I want money and only the Palme d'Or attracts money.'

George Cukor, who in a classic case of unlike poles attracting expressed his admiration for *Journal* and offered help in getting the film distributed, as it eventually was, in the United States (Ehrenstein 1996: 103). More than ten years later, in 1964, Bresson wrote to Cukor saying that he would like to film *Lancelot* in English, with Natalie Wood and Burt Lancaster who seemed to him the very incarnation of the hero. The project fell through, Lancaster already being committed to shooting Frankenheimer's *The Train*. The least that can be said is that such a film would be very difficult to imagine, if only because Bresson had abjured professional actors twenty years before and his *modus operandi* could scarcely have been more different from what Lancaster and Wood would have been used to. John Waters, an unlikely Bressonian if ever there were, says of *Lancelot*: 'If ever there was an anti-star movie, this is it', on the ground that 'although it seems like a cast of thousands, it is actually only a handful playing many different roles' (Waters 1998: 589). By 1974, Bresson was on more familiar ground, using unknown *modèles* (Luc Simon as Lancelot, Laura Duke Condominas as Guenièvre and Humbert Balsan, later to be his assistant on *Le Diable probablement*, as Gauvain) who often seem to quote their lines rather than speaking them – a familiar Bressonian strategy that reinforces our sense of the film's intertextuality and makes it impossible to read the film, like in a totally different way Rohmer's *Perceval le Gallois* of four years later, as in any sense a 'realist' work.

To speak of a 'sense of period' in *Lancelot*, as commentators on films set in the distant past often do, would, of course, be an oxymoron. Julien Gracq evokes 'ce qu'on n'ose pas tout à fait appeler, tant les deux mots jurent d'être accolés, son réalisme arthurien'[2] (Gracq 1997: 56). The Arthurian legends have been a staple of Western European culture from the thirteenth century through to modern times (Cocteau's play *Les Chevaliers de la table ronde* or indeed *Monty Python and the Holy Grail*), but their status as, precisely, legend means that it is impossible to situate them chronologically. Jean-Pierre Jeancolas frequently uses the term

2 'what I dare not call outright, so flagrantly do the two words clash, its Arthurian realism.'

'contemporain vague'('vaguely contemporary') to refer to many modern films; it would be possible in the same way to speak of a 'médiéval vague' ('vaguely medieval') spanning such diverse phenomena as Viollet-le-Duc's restoration of the walled city of Carcassonne and Jean-Marie Poiré's 1993 film comedy *Les Visiteurs*. Kristin Thompson points out that the film's characters 'are far too young to have lived through all the triumphs of the Round Table and to be now in a late period of decline' (Thompson 1998: 347–8) – a further indication of how radically outside historical, or even biological, time *Lancelot* is. The 'realism' to which Gracq refers resides paradoxically in *Lancelot*'s construction of 'une histoire qui n'a jamais eu ni modèle, ni lieu réel, qui n'a jamais connu dès sa naissance d'autre climat que celui du mythe, ni d'autre séjour que les ailes de l'imagination'[3] (Gracq 1997: 56). What might the determinants of such an atemporal realism be?

Primary among them, and of great importance in *Lancelot*, is the representation of what might be called a 'pre-modern' body, which the hieratic, two-dimensional quality of much medieval painting, and later the jovially euphemistic stylisation of Hollywood representations of the Middle Ages (Curtiz and Keighley's *The Adventures of Robin Hood* is a good example), had the effect of occluding. Recent cinematic representations, from Pasolini's *The Decameron* and *The Canterbury Tales* through to the aforementioned *Les Visiteurs*, have reinscribed the 'pre-modern' body, one whose drives and appetites are not (yet) subject to the societal and hygienic restraints of modernity. The films I have mentioned deploy this body to largely comic effect in a manner often spoken of as 'Rabelaisian'. Bakhtin, however, is there to remind us that for Rabelais's 'grotesque realism', 'life and death, birth, excrement, and food are all drawn together and tied in one grotesque knot' – a more complex, even tragic, vision than Rabelais is often credited with. That grotesqueness expresses 'the ambivalence of the material bodily lower stratum, which destroys and generates, swallows and is swallowed' (Bakhtin 1994: 215). The lewd and the

---

3 'a (hi)story that has never had a model nor known a real place, that since its birth has known no other climate than that of myth, nor any resting-place than the wings of imagination.'

excremental, it should by now be clear, do not belong in Bresson's work, yet the number of shots of legs and feet, human or equine, in *Lancelot* suggest that the specificity of his 'pre-modern' body is nevertheless reliant on its 'lower stratum', deprived of its comic possibilities through being encased in armour and thereby much more starkly close to tragedy than Rabelais's ambivalence.

The quantities of blood that gush from beneath the slaughtered knights' armour in the film's opening and closing sequences provide the most striking instance of that body as tragic, its urges incorporating – or here excorporating – the death drive Thanatos that is so important in Bresson's work.[4] They shock in a very different way from far bloodier episodes in Peckinpah or Tarantino, by the textural contrast between the spouting gore and the metallic sheen of the armour and by the absence of a visible human body – a 'modern' body? – from which the blood might flow.[5] When Michel Mesnil writes that 'ici on perd son sang comme on pisse, à la lettre on pisse le sang',[6] it is the impersonality of the 'on' that shocks as much as the bawdiness of 'pisse'. Vital to *Lancelot*'s construction of the body in a completely opposite way is its place in courtly love, analysed by Denis de Rougemont in *L'Amour et l'occident* (1972). Courtly love assigned to a lady her knight, dedicated to her service and the bearer of her insignia in jousts, but bound by the iron rule which 's'oppose à ce qu'une telle passion "tourne à la réalité", c'est-à-dire aboutissant à "l'entière possession de sa dame"' (de Rougemont 1972: 25).[7] The biological body, in other words, was figured in courtly love but by the same token excluded from it. Such a passion breaks its own law in the two most famous Arthurian legends – that of Tristan and Iseult and that of Lancelot and Guinevere. Once that rule is broken – once, in Lacanian terms, the biological phallus displaces its law-giving symbolic other – death is the usurping body's inevitable

4 See above, p. 118.
5 Uccello's paintings of the battle of San Romano dehumanise their combattants' bodies in a similar way.
6 'here one loses one's blood just as one pisses, one literally pisses blood.'
7 '[which] is opposed to such a passion's "becoming reality", in other words leading to "the complete possession of one's lady".'

fate. That necessary relationship between love and death, central to this day in western culture, finds its artistic apotheosis in the *Liebestod* which concludes Wagner's *Tristan and Isolde*. *Lancelot* also sets before us such a relationship, but one driven by entropy not ecstasy. culminating in the clattering Dürer-like pile of what can only be called dead suits of armour in the final shot. To understand why this has to be so, we have to turn paradoxically to that very history whose foreclosure we have seen to be the necessary condition of the film's 'réalisme arthurien'.

That foreclosure is overturned in the very final sequence, when archers perched in the trees shoot dead King Arthus and his remaining knights. The archers are not, individually or as a group, identified, nor is there any narrative preparation for their assault. The shock it induces is intensified by the abrupt sense of a world and a style of combat in its death agony. As Sémolué says, 'les archers juchés dans les arbres annoncent un changement de société dû à l'évolution de l'Histoire: le temps des chevaliers et des tournois est révolu'[8] (Sémolué 1993: 225). History, lurking in ambush, has destroyed the time of myth, making this the most cosmically pessimistic of Bresson's endings. It echoes, like *Un condamné*, Renoir's *La Grande Illusion*, a radically different type of film but one also sustained by a tragic awareness that more ruthless methods of warfare are destroying the principles and practice of chivalry.

That destruction is already present in *Lancelot*'s opening shots – knights killing and decapitating one another, fire laying land to waste, the consecrated objects on an altar swept to the ground with a flourish of the sword. The vanity of the search for the Grail, to which the introductory titles will shortly allude, here becomes shockingly plain. Just as surely as when the husband in *Une femme douce* buys the golden surround of the wife's crucifix and discards the ivory Christ, the spiritual value of the artefacts of religion is brushed aside. It is difficult not to see, in this period film preceded and followed by works harshly critical of the modern world, contemporary overtones to the despairing

8 'the archers perched in the trees herald a change of society caused by the unfolding of History: the time of knighthood and of tournaments is finished.'

barbarity of Bresson's knights, as to that of their Teutonic counterparts in Eisenstein's *Alexander Nevsky* (1938).

The symmetrical apocalypses of beginning and end suggest a further way in which the action of *Lancelot* is situated outside historical or chronological time, well articulated by John Pruitt:

> The action can be seen perhaps as not an unfolding narrative so much as a static analysis of a single moment in which a society loses its ways, and instantly dissipates and dies. The circularity of the film (as in *Pickpocket*) is a kind of denial of temporal progression and puts the action into a ritualised, symbolic realm, the end of which is sealed right at the beginning. (Pruitt 1985: 8)

In *Une femme douce* too 'the end ... is sealed right at the beginning', by way of a flashback structure perhaps more oppressive, but less cosmic in its implications, than that of *Lancelot*, whose warriors seem trapped in a nightmare of eternal recurrence (the Nietzschean first cousin to Thanatos). After the introductory titles, we hear the galloping of a horse and see an old peasant woman asserting that anybody whose steps are heard before he is seen is soon to die, even if the steps are those of his horse – at once a premonition of the fatal ambush at the end and an ironic assertion of Bresson's promotion of sound over image. No sooner have these words been spoken than Lancelot rides into view. He arrives at Arthus's castle and is reunited with the King and Gauvain. Later (it is, unsurprisingly, difficult, and probably irrelevant, to tell how much time passes between sequences in this film), he emerges from his tent and asks if it is time for Mass. The reply ('Les trois coups n'ont pas encore sonné')[9] evokes the 'trois coups' that traditionally herald the beginning of a performance in French classical theatre. After the sacrilegious onslaught of the opening images, the Mass is now assimilated to a theatrical performance – in the light of Bresson's strictures on filmed theatre a further ironic undercutting of the Christian values whose dissolution is the tragic subject of the film.

The first meeting between Lancelot and Guenièvre, whose lover he has vowed no longer to be, is filmed fairly flatly in shot/

9 'The three blows have not yet been struck/the bell has not rung three times.'

reverse-shot. The variation of types of shot and camera distance in this film is greater than in much of Bresson, though facial close-ups (except of horses) are comparatively rare. Shot/reverse-shot is characteristic of confrontation, a classic cinematic device for the maintenance of tension. That tension between the carnal and the spiritual is reinforced here by the cold tones in which the lovers speak, as though in quotation marks. The exchange between Guenièvre and Lancelot when he tells her of his vow ('Tu as fait ça? – Je l'ai fait')[10] evokes the laconicism of some of the exchanges between Jeanne and Michel in *Pickpocket*, the intensity of the emotions at stake thrown into relief by the detached tone of their utterance. At Mass, Guenièvre gazes at Lancelot, the sacred ceremony becoming a theatre of desire as it has done in a very different social context in *Balthazar*.

It is in the following scene that we see the Round Table for the first and only time, as Arthus announces his decision to close off the room it is in – the film's most explicit recognition that the age of chivalrous community is dead. The exchange between Arthus and Gauvain ('Mon oncle, il faut faire quelque chose. Donnez-nous un but. – Il faut prier. – Prier?')[11] calls to mind the crisis of prayer so important in *Journal*. There is, however, an important difference; in the earlier film, that crisis is, precisely, the priest's alone, and it is in passing through it that he attains what we finally recognise to be his salvation. *Lancelot* situates the crisis as one of an entire civilisation (the violated altar at the beginning has suggested as much), and proffers no form of answer to it. Lancelot is to be shown praying at the altar for God not to abandon him and those loyal to Arthus, but the prayer is evidently in vain.

Knight and queen meet again as the full moon shines, Guenièvre pleading for love and leaving her white scarf behind on a bench as though to emphasise her kinship with the *femme douce*. In this scene we see them, for the first time, in the same shot, the camera suggesting the bodily *rapprochement* that is taking place. Mordred – as his very name suggests the villain of the piece – takes the scarf to his tent, where Lancelot goes to meet him. In

10 'You have done that? – I have.'
11 'Uncle, we must do something. Give us a goal. – We must pray. – Pray?'

another shot/reverse-shot sequence, Mordred ignores Lancelot's outstretched hand, another in the long Bressonian series of utterances or gestures that remain without a reply. Gauvain finds it extraordinary that Lancelot has endured this insult, and tells him that many knights, including Gauvain's own brother Agravain, have gone over to the enemy. Knights arrive from Escalot challenging Arthus's men to a tournament, for which we then see them training. Gauvain, like Lancelot and the others transfixed by the light from Guenièvre's window, speaks of her as 'notre seule femme, notre soleil'[12] – all too literally true in this film in which the only other women we see are the old peasant and the young girl in the woods. The training and tournament scenes that follow emphasise the bleakly androcentric world in which the knights live, a world seemingly without the wherewithal for its biological as well as its cultural and symbolic renewal.

Lancelot's next assignation with Guenièvre is all the more powerful in consequence. The queen instructs him: 'Prends ce corps interdit'[13] – a phrase with sacrilegious overtones of the Last Supper, and thus of the Grail whose vain quest has brought the Arthurian world to the brink of despair. It is that forbidden body – sensual, sexual, in a word, corporeal – that she passionately asserts in the love scene when, spied upon by Mordred, she exhorts Lancelot: 'Serre-moi, je ne suis pas un fantôme'.[14] This reinstatement of a body proscribed finds its necessary consequence and counterpart in the bodies butchered at the end, 'fantômes' if ever there were. Religion may be of as little help in this film as anywhere else in Bresson, but the economy of Catholicism is none the less inexorably at work.

Lancelot, yielding to Guenièvre's entreaties, announces that he will not fight in the tournament. As Arthus's troops set off we see only the feet of the horses – Bakhtin's 'material bodily lower stratum' reinscribed as in another way it has been in the love scene, an omen too of their riderlessness to come. We see Guenièvre being bathed by her attendants, a remarkable scene because of the total

---

12 'our only woman, our sun.'
13 'Take this forbidden body.'
14 'Hold me, I am not a ghost.'

immobility that makes her 'nude' (in the artistic sense) rather than naked, thereby contrasting with the love scene. Lancelot, in a belated pre-Cornelian assertion of the primacy of duty over love, orders his horse to be saddled for the tournament, where he fights anonymously, but is identified by his combative skill. The tournament sequence is one of the only passages in Bresson, along with the Gare de Lyon scene in *Pickpocket*, that might be described as bravura. Yet that word's connotations of gratuitous display are foreign to it, for it is the structural centre of the film (Thompson 1998: 360), and the dismemberment of the body and the regular aural and visual rhythms that are its most conspicuous features both serve clearly defined purposes. The fighting is scanned by the hoisting of banners and the repeated skirling of bagpipes to suggest for the only time in the film a world moving in conformity to the rhythm of its own rules, a microcosm immune to the disorder and worse looming outside. The close-ups of lances, hooves and armour both portend the bloody dismemberment to come and more generally emphasise how much *Lancelot* is a film of the body – social, sacred, grotesque – in crisis, unable to function or perceive itself as any kind of whole. Beneath the excitement of this sequence lie the germs of tragedy.

That tragedy is foreshadowed by the abrupt departure of Lancelot, who collapses wounded in the forest. Guenièvre weeps for him. We discover that he is being protected by the old woman we saw at the beginning predicting his death. She tries to persuade him not to leave, but, covered in blood, he returns, Tristan-like, to Guenièvre, whom he carries off, unwittingly killing Agravain and fatally wounding Gauvain himself. The Round Table's prime defender is now the agent of its destruction.

Arthus agrees to take back Guenièvre, professing to believe her innocent. In one of the film's most remarkable images, we see Lancelot and Guenièvre walking in extremely long shot towards Arthus's tent; the king takes her hand and goes with her into the tent, after which she is not seen again. Giorgio Tinazzi's description of *Lancelot* as a 'recapitulation ... of the major lines of Bresson's cinema' (Tinazzi 1975 [my translation]: 83) may seem curious given the film's setting, yet one respect in which it plainly rings true is the recurrent theme of the woman who disappears from the film. We never find out what becomes of Hélène in *Les Dames*, of Chantal in *Journal* or of Marie in *Balthazar*. The three otherwise different women have in common that they have been plunged into (Hélène, Marie) or – perhaps – just emerged from (Chantal) a crisis that has put or may put the very foundation of their being at risk. That Guenièvre goes into Arthus's tent never to emerge has overtones all the more ominous if we think too of the *femme douce*'s promise of conjugal fidelity immediately before her suicide.

In the final sequence, Lancelot learns that Mordred is leading an uprising, and asserts his fealty with a cry of support for Arthus. The knights gallop off into the carnage and chaos of the final shots – smoke (what is burning?) spirals above the trees, a falcon hovers, perhaps vulture-like, in a recurrent image, a deranged and riderless horse (whose was it?) passes several times, the unidentified archers wreak their havoc. The king's armour, its helmet bearing his crown, is one of a lifeless pile on the ground. Lancelot's dying word is: 'Guenièvre!' – an assertion of profane over courtly love, and thus a final betrayal of the chivalrous ideal, but one which matters hardly at all, for there is nobody to hear it. Bresson's nearest approach to an action film ends in total silence.

References

Bakhtin, Mikhail (1994), 'Carnival Ambivalence: Laughter, Praise and Abuse', in Pam Morris (ed.), *The Bakhtin Reader*, London and New York, Arnold.

Ehrenstein, David (1996), 'Bresson et Cukor: histoire d'une correspondance', *Positif*, no. 430.

Gracq, Julien (1997), '*Lancelot du lac*', in *Robert Bresson: Éloge*, Milan and Paris, Mazzotta/Cinémathèque française.

Pruitt, John (1985), 'Robert Bresson's *Lancelot du lac*', *Field of Vision*, no. 13.

Sémolué, Jean (1993), *Bresson ou l'acte pur des métamorphoses*, Paris, Flammarion.

Thompson, Kristin (1998), 'The Sheen of Armour, the Whinnies of Horses: Sparse Parametric Style in *Lancelot du Lac*', in James Quandt (ed.), *Robert Bresson*, Toronto, Cinematheque Ontario.

Tinazzi, Giorgio (1975), *Il Cinema di Robert Bresson*, Venice, Marsilo.

Waters, John (1998), in James Quandt (ed.), *Robert Bresson*, Cinematheque Ontario, Toronto.

7

The director as writer: *Notes sur le cinématographe*

Bresson's *Notes sur le cinématographe*, first published in 1975 and reissued in 1988 with a short preface by the novelist J. M. G. le Clézio, distils a quarter-century's reflection upon the principles and practice of cinematography. It is quite common for European film-makers in particular to write about cinema, but generally in the form of either journalistic articles (as with the criticism of Truffaut, Godard and the other *Cahiers* writers), or attempts at constructing a theory of cinema (Eisenstein, Pasolini). *Notes sur le cinématographe* (hereinafter *Notes*) – as much *sui generis* as its author's films – fits into neither of these categories, and indeed could even be said not to be about 'cinema' at all, which for Bresson is the contrary of cinematography. The text takes the form of a series of aphoristic fragments or maxims, most dating from between 1950 and 1958 with a smaller number from between 1960 and 1974. The aphoristic tradition is a particularly strong one in French writing, largely because of its proximity to Latin; La Rochefoucauld and Chamfort are among its best-known exemplars, though more relevant than either to Bresson's work, as we have seen, is Pascal, above all in the *Pensées*. Another name much cited in *Notes* is that of Montaigne, whose *Essais* represent the first-known use of that term to refer to a published text, and thus for all their discursive coherence remain in one sense at least 'attempts' or 'drafts'.

Bresson's views on cinematic theory are nowhere recorded, but it is a fairly safe bet that he would view its practitioners much as

Pascal did those of whom he says, in a passage quoted in *Notes*, '*Ils veulent trouver la solution là où tout n'est qu'énigme*'[1] (84) (all subsequent quotations in this chapter will be from *Notes* unless otherwise stated). Le Clézio compares *Notes* to the woodblock paintings of the late eighteenth- and early nineteenth-century Japanese master Hokusai (9). Those paintings are impregnated with the Zen tradition from which sprang the *koan* and the *haiku*, the paradoxical riddle without solution and the tersely epigrammatic verse, in their turn evoked by Roland Barthes in *Fragments d'un discours amoureux* (1977). The 1970s were also a period in which French intellectual life was greatly influenced by the work of Nietzsche and Heidegger – both exponents of the aphoristic mode, though Heidegger is anything but terse. Bresson, unlike Godard, has always remained in his public persona, at any rate, aloof from the world of Parisian intellectualism, yet it is difficult not to detect in *Notes* the impact of those wider – or narrower – concerns.

The major preoccupations of *Notes* will come as no surprise to anybody familiar with Bresson: a polemical rejection of cinema in favour of cinematography and of the actor in favour of the *modèle*, a pervasive interest in painting (El Greco and Cézanne in particular), a stress on the pared down and the minimalist ('La faculté de bien me servir de mes moyens diminue lorsque leur nombre augmente'[2] (15)). His description of the '*deux morts et ... trois naissances*' that go to make up his films suggests why he is unwilling to use the same *modèle* twice:

> Mon film naît une première fois dans ma tête, meurt sur papier; est ressuscité par les personnes vivantes et les objets réels que j'emploie, qui sont tués sur pellicule mais qui, placés dans un certain ordre et projetés sur un écran, se raniment comme des fleurs dans l'eau.[3] (25)

1 'They want to find a solution where everything is an enigma.'
2 'The ability to make good use of my means declines when they become more abundant.'
3 '*two deaths and ... three births*' ... 'My film is born for the first time in my head and dies on paper. It is resurrected by the living persons and the real objects I use, killed on film but coming alive again like flowers in water once they are placed in a certain order and projected onto a screen.'

The stress here on Bresson's need to 'kill the thing he loves' – object or *modèle* – and on the importance of editing to bring it back to life reflects the twofold powerlessness, over their 'performance' and the use made of it in the finished film, often enough attested to by those who have worked with him. He refers in this connection to the importance of automatism, calling Montaigne in evidence (*'Tout mouvement nous descouvre* [Montaigne]. Mais il ne nous découvre que s'il est automatique [non commandé, non voulu]')[4] (130). Arnaud, following Lacan, refers to automatism as that mode of pure contingency in which we encounter, for the vocabulary of religious transcendence, destiny and, for that of psychoanalysis, the 'real' (Arnaud 1986: 34–5). It is, in other words, that which escapes the conscious control of the ego to reveal the impulses and drives beneath (*Pickpocket*, as so often in this connection, is the clearest example in Bresson's *œuvre*).[5] In this sense we can speak of the role of the *modèle* as analogous to that of the analysand, so that 'le film répète en un autre sens la situation du tournage qui en est la miniature'[6] (Arnaud 1986: 35), in a partial effacement of the distinction between on- and off-screen persona.

Bresson's strictures on music in the section entitled 'De la musique' may appear surprising if we think of his use of Mozart in *Un condamné* or of Monteverdi at the end of *Mouchette*. Yet, as we have seen, non-diegetic music disappears from his work after *Mouchette*, almost as though the advent of colour called for some kind of counterbalancing ascesis. 'Il faut que les bruits deviennent musique'[7] (32); the intercutting of Schubert and the donkey braying at the start of *Balthazar* is perhaps the most audacious example of this in the director's work, though as we have seen there are many more.

The section entitled 'De l'automatisme' is the clearest justi-fication of Bresson's allegiance to *modèles* rather than actors. Once

4 *'Any movement reveals us* [Montaigne]. But it reveals us only if it is automatic (neither commanded nor willed).'
5 See above, pp. 52–61.
6 'the film repeats in a different way the situation of its shooting, which represents it on a smaller scale.'
7 'Noises must become music.'

modèles' behaviour has become automatic – a goal generally achieved through constant repetition – 'leurs rapports avec les personnes et les objets autour d'eux seront *justes*, parce qu'ils ne seront pas *pensés*'[8] (34–5). Here again the importance of bypassing the control of the ego, in cinematography as in psychoanalysis, is seen as fundamental. What the *modèle* gives the film-maker is defined as a '*substance*' (41) – something like the kernel of his or her being, akin to Christian conceptions of the uniqueness of the individual soul. Thus it is that 'TES MODÈLES, UNE FOIS SORTIS D'EUX-MÊMES, NE POURRONT PLUS Y RENTRER'[9] (54) – whence the almost literal unthinkability of using the same *modèle* twice.

Closely connected with Bresson's philosophy of the *modèle*, and, like it, manifesting affinities with the psychoanalytic process, is the importance he gives to silence as a substantive part of film-making ('Trouver une parenté entre image, son et silence'[10] (59)). Shortly after this is to be found his celebrated dictum: 'Lorsqu'un son peut remplacer une image, supprimer l'image ou la neutraliser'[11] (62), which suggests a hierarchy in which sound is superior to image and silence to either. We may be reminded here of the celebrated closing line of Wittgenstein's *Tractatus* ('Whereof one cannot speak, thereof one must be silent' (Wittgenstein [1921] 1983: 189)) – a maxim that can be said to underlie much of Bresson's work.

Bresson speaks of the real, in terms curiously evocative of Lacan, as that which 'arrivé à notre esprit n'est déja plus du réel'[12] (79) – that which, in other words, is constitutively inaccessible as such, that whereof in the most literal sense one cannot but be silent though/because it is the necessary horizon of any textuality at all. That real is to be found in the words and gestures of Bresson's *modèles*, who are expressive in spite of themselves, '[m]odèles expressifs involontaires (et non pas inexpressifs

8 'Their relationships with the people and objects around them will be *truthful* because they will not be *thought out*.'
9 'YOUR MODÈLES, ONCE THEY HAVE EMERGED FROM THEMSELVES, WILL NOT BE ABLE TO GET BACK AGAIN.'
10 'Find a kinship between image, sound and silence.'
11 'When a sound can replace an image, get rid of the image or neutralise it.'
12 'when it reaches our mind, it is already no longer the real.'

volontaires)'[13] (81). The countenance of Michel in *Pickpocket*, the irony with which the words of the *femme douce*'s husband are imbued in spite of himself, even – especially? – Balthazar's lying down to die, distil this paradox, fundamental to the whole notion of the Bressonian *modèle*.

The section entitled 'Exercices' evokes the *Spiritual Exercises* of St Ignatius Loyola – for Barthes, the work that established the primacy of sight over hearing in the western spiritual tradition, and one remarkable for its *mise en scène* of the body. The 'masse de désir qui s'agite' (Barthes 1971: 67) in the *Exercises* finds an echo both in Oudart's arraigning of Bresson for his sadistic urges towards his *modèles* and, less censoriously, in the films' marshalling of bodily desires against themselves – Lancelot's for Guenièvre, Michel's for proscribed homosocial contact, the country priest's for a wholeness that is to be his only in the moment of death. The Greek Catholic injunction '"Soyez attentifs!"' is counterposed to 'CINÉMA', which, along with other popular media, is an 'école d'inattention'.[14] What are we to be attentive to? An answer comes in *Notes*' final section, which speaks not of the beautiful images of a film ('cartepostalisme') but of 'l'ineffable qu'elles dégageront'[15] (119). Yet that ineffable – the Bressonian divine? – remains stubbornly material, as the work's very final paragraph demonstrates:

> DIVINATION, ce nom, comment ne pas l'associer aux deux machines sublimes dont je me sers pour travailler? Caméra et magnétophone, emmenez-moi loin de l'intelligence qui complique tout.[16] (138)

Laborare est orare, indeed, applied with self-transcending artisanal humility to the tools of the cinematographer's trade. Nowhere in Bresson's work is 'l'intelligence qui complique tout' more obviously the enemy than in his next (and penultimate) film, *Le Diable probablement*, to which we shall now turn.

---

13 'involuntarily expressive *modèles*, not voluntarily inexpressive ones.'
14 '"Be attentive!"' ... 'A school of unattentiveness.'
15 'A picture-postcard aesthetic ... the ineffable that emanates from them.'
16 'DIVINATION – how can I not associate that name with the two sublime machines I use in my work? Camera and tape-recorder, take me far away from understanding and its endless complications.'

References

Arnaud, Phillippe (1986), *Robert Bresson*, Paris, Cahiers du cinema.

Barthes, Roland (1971), *Sade, Fourier, Loyola*, Paris, Seuil.

Bresson, Robert ([1975] 1988), *Notes sur le cinématographe*, Paris, Gallimard.

Estève, Michel (1983), *Robert Bresson: la passion du cinématographe*, Paris, Albatros.

Wittgenstein, Ludwig ([1921] 1983), *Tractatus Logico-Philosophicus*, London and New York, Routledge.

8

Civilisation and its discontents: *Le Diable probablement* and *L'Argent*

We have often enough seen how important the death-drive, Thanatos, is for Bresson's work. Freud's *Civilisation and its Discontents* describes 'the struggle between Eros and Death, between the instinct of life and the instinct of destruction' as 'what all life essentially consists of' (Freud [1930] 1961: 82), and Bresson's last two films foreground that struggle with particular force. *L'Argent*, adapted from Tolstoy's novella *The Forged Coupon*, ends on a note of ambiguity that might be called Dostoevskyan, whereas *Le Diable probablement* (hereinafter *Le Diable*) concludes with the virtually unequivocal triumph of Thanatos – a triumph scarcely in doubt right from the beginning.

Le Diable's very title suggests the pessimism of its outcome. We hear the phrase when Charles, the film's suicidal 'hero', and his long-suffering friend Michel are on a bus; a conversation among the *passengers* leads one of them to ask: 'Qui nous manœuvre en douce?' to which another replies: 'Le diable probablement',[1] at which point the bus collides noisily with another vehicle. Bresson claims (*L'Express*, 1977) to have felt the Devil's presence on two (unspecified) occasions in his life, but belief in a personal devil ('Satan') nowadays tends to be the province of fundamentalist Protestants rather than Catholics, whose disengagement from it can be traced back as far as Augustine for whom 'evil has no existence except as a privation of good' (Augustine [397] 1992: 43).

---

1 'Who is manipulating us on the quiet?' ... 'The devil, probably.'

Such a view is entirely consonant with Bresson's film, which unlike *Balthazar* or *Lancelot* has no obviously evil character, but within whose world the 'privation of good' seems all but total. Religion, politics, psychoanalysis – the major institutionalisations of the drive towards a better life – are each in turn shown to be inadequate, and Serge Daney's observation that 'jamais il [sc. Bresson] n'a marqué aussi rageusement, aussi radicalement, le mépris dans lequel il tient *tout* discours'[2] (Daney, 1996: 163) distils the nihilism at work within the film. If 'la voix bresson-ienne est celle qui nécessite d'ouvrir la bouche *au minimum*'[3] (Daney 1996: 175), that is the corollary, in this film especially, of the pointlessness of the words it proffers. Nor do personal relationships offer any more hope. The skein of love affairs and friendships that might appear to knit the central group together does no such thing, for 'les personnages se laissent aller d'un côté, puis de l'autre'[4] (Sémolué 1993: 236), prey to an inertia or *accidie* to which Catholic theology is no stranger, but which in the world of *Le Diable* suggests the disillusionment and loss of purpose increasingly marked in France once the utopian visions of May 1968 had faded. To this extent *Le Diable* is, more than any other Bresson, a film of its time – something suggested by the director when he explained: 'Ce qui m'a poussé à faire ce film c'est le gâchis qu'on a fait de tout'[5] (*Quotidien de Paris* 16 June 1977: 9).

The film, shot in Paris during the intense summer heatwave of 1976, had a chequered early career. The commission that allocates advance funding (*avance sur recettes*) to directors voted against doing so to Bresson, who was able to make the film only after the personal intervention of the Culture Minister, Michel Guy. It did not form part of the official selection for the 1977 Cannes Festival and Bresson refused to have it shown in the Directors' Fortnight, the major 'fringe' event, saying that he no longer liked Cannes because of its polluted waters (presumably in more senses than

2 'never has Bresson so angrily and radically shown the contempt he has for *any* discourse.'
3 'the Bressonian voice reduces the need to open one's mouth *to a minimum*.'
4 'the characters drift first this way, then that.'
5 'What drove me to make this film was the way we waste and spoil everything.'

one). Initially it was authorised to be shown only to those over eighteen years of age, and it was not until after much pressure had been brought to bear that this decision was rescinded. It shared the Silver Bear second prize at the Berlin Festival only after the German director Fassbinder and the British critic Derek Malcolm had threatened to leave the jury if their support for it were not made public. Fassbinder's praise for the film and its characters' 'rejecting every commitment' (Fassbinder 1998: 550) echoes Daney's view, and was to be mirrored in the growing nihilism of his own later work, in other respects so unlike that of Bresson.

More recent films about the problems of young people in France – Matthieu Kassowitz's *La Haine* of 1995 is the best known – have tended to have settings far more materially deprived than the cosseted 'BCBG'[6] world of Bresson's main characters, seemingly frozen somewhere between school, university and the 'real' world in which the only one who has any kind of project is the aspirant ecologist author, Michel. None has any evident material worries except the heroin-addicted Valentin, whose name like those of Alberte and the sports-car-driving Edwige evokes a well-off, even slightly old-fashioned social milieu, redolent perhaps of Proust. (The bus on which the Devil is invoked is a number 22, which serves the up-market sixteenth *arrondissement* of Paris – one of the very few topographical indications in the film.) Yet the cultural upheaval of 1968 and the years after made it dramatically clear that much of the greatest personal dissatisfaction, even misery, was to be found precisely among groups such as this, where economic affluence and emotional deprivation often went hand in hand. Carax's *Les Amants du Pont Neuf* of 1991, already referred to in our discussion of *Quatre nuits*,[7] gives a far more stylised evocation of the world we see on the banks of the Seine in *Le Diable*, where the well-off young seek solace or excitement in the company of *zonards* ('drop-outs'). Charles's father, we learn in his interview with the psychoanalyst, is a well-off provincial tree-felling contractor; but Charles's early life was marred by numerous beatings, which have marked him

6 See above, p. 106.
7 See above, p. 108.

emotionally. The fact that we never see the parents of any of the central characters at least hints at a dysfunctionality and absence of warmth most clearly seen when Alberte cavalierly empties the family refrigerator. Truffaut's view that the film is really about 'l'intelligence, la gravité et la beauté des adolescents d'aujourd'hui'[8] (Truffaut and Lantil-Le Dantec 1997: 59) seems to me valid only if the qualities he mentions are perceived in the truly tragic light in which Bresson shows them.

Le Diable is a tragedy played out above all through the body. The chain of sexual desire and rejection that links the four main characters (and to which a fifth, an unnamed young woman, is fleetingly added) is for Jean-Pierre Oudart driven by an 'obsession du corps adorable' whose narcissism is only apparent, not even negative. Negative narcissism would reside in the dandyistic paradox 'je serais niais de m'aimer moi-même', whereas 'le corps bressonien ne cesse de proférer: tu serais niais de m'adorer'[9] (Oudart 1977: 28–9). Shots of the lower body, omitting the head and shoulders, are common in this film, as in the early scene in which the group discuss the best way to walk (a curious echo, though the phrase is not actually spoken, of Claude Miller's La Meilleure Façon de marcher, from two years before). The almost philosophical seriousness with which this question is invested, complete with rigorous scrutiny of the sole of each character's shoes, appears almost ludicrous – an impression strengthened by the flared trousers they all wear. But this scene, like all that follow, acquires a properly tragic dimension through being viewed in retrospect, for the credits have been followed by shots of newspaper headlines referring to Charles's suicide or murder. Like Une femme douce, Le Diable allows us no room for doubt about its outcome.

The group of friends then take themselves off to a political meeting, albeit a highly implausible one. Even the giddiest post-1968 rhetoric was unlikely to yield a public speech beginning: 'Je proclame la destruction'[10] – a phrase more evocative of the nihil-

8 'The intelligence, the gravity and the beauty of today's adolescents.'
9 'I should be stupid to love myself' ... 'You would be stupid to love/worship me.'
10 'I proclaim destruction.'

ists in Dostoevsky's *The Devils* (also known as *The Possessed*), whose rage to destroy conceals the deep spiritual unhappiness that drives one of their number, Kirilov, to suicide. One of the characters in Godard's *La Chinoise*, made in 1967 but astonishingly prophetic of the 'spirit of 1968', also bears the name Kirilov, so that his suicide in that film comes as no surprise. The deflating of the wilder hopes raised by 1968 led to a number of suicides, as well as a steady trek to the psychoanalyst's couch and for many a return to some form of religious faith, so that in these respects *Le Diable* again proves to be a highly contemporary film.

Charles succeeds in being even more nihilistic than the speaker when he describes the militants as 'des cons, tous des cons',[11] and the friends leave the meeting. In the next sequence, we see Michel and two fellow students watching what is still quite horrifying footage of environmental pollution, indicting the destruction of entire species for profit. 'The environment' in 1977 was not the universal object of concern it is today; the first French Green Party was not formed until 1984, so that Bresson shows himself here to be ahead of his time. Alberte leaves the family home to join Charles, with whom she is going to live. Michel – who loves her and whom she in her turn claims to love – pleads with her not to go ('Tu vas faire mourir tes parents de chagrin. – Je n'y peux rien').[12] We are reminded of the Bressonian woman – Marie, Marthe – powerless before the claims of a lover on whom she cannot even fully rely. Edwige, a rival of Alberte's for Charles's affections though clearly not a hostile one, drives him to his flat, a slightly larger but still fairly run-down version of Michel's room in *Pickpocket*. We suspect that any broken hearts sustained by Alberte's parents will be the result of class consciousness as much as of concern for her emotional welfare.

The following scene illustrates the inadequacy of religious discourse much as the meeting scene has done that of the political. The group of friends find themselves in a church where a discussion group is gathered. The group's concern for the poor

---

11 'shitheads, the lot of them.'
12 'You'll break your parents' hearts. – There's nothing I can do about that.'

and the oppressed, like the proclamation of one of its members that the Christianity of the future will be without religion, suggests that it is allied with the radical, even revolutionary Catholicism that came to the fore during and after 1968. The poor and oppressed were the central focus of the liberation theology so influential in Latin America, while the remark on religion, excessive though it may sound, could well have been taken from the work of the heterodox Lutheran theologian Rudolf Bultmann. The content of this discourse, then, seems more plausible than that of the political meeting; but content is perhaps less important here than contempt, that contempt in which Daney has said Bresson holds any discourse at all – a contempt traceable back to Dufréty's self-justifying verbiage near the end of *Journal*, and here articulated by the soundtrack. The words of the debate – 'une suite de questions n'attendant ni réponse, ni réplique'[13] (Daney 1996: 163) – are punctuated by the raucous honking of the organ being tuned and the sound of a vacuum-cleaner sweeping across the church carpet. The organ might be seen, in a more sympathetic perspective than Daney's, as analogous to the rethinking and 'retuning' of Christianity to which the group's discussion clearly aspires, while in the same light the vacuum-cleaner may evoke the adage 'laborare est orare' and the George Herbert poem mentioned in our discussion of *Un condamné*.[14] Yet there is a negativity to Bresson's use of sound in this film at variance with much of the earlier work, illustrated by Daney's assertion that the noise of the trees sawed down (by Charles's father's firm?) 'rend *a priori* tout débat *inutile puisque inaudible*'[15] (Daney 1996: 166). The vacuum-cleaner, while far less noisy than either the debate or the organ, for Daney wrecks the symmetrical opposition between them – thus, any spiritual value we might be tempted to ascribe to the scene – by introducing an element of triviality. To this I would add that it works intertextually too, as a muted, technologically neutered echo of the rake in the great *Journal* scene between the priest and the countess. In that scene, as we have seen, the noise

13 'a string of questions expecting neither reply nor retort.'
14 See above, p. 47.
15 'makes any debate necessarily *pointless since it cannot be heard*.'

of raking – a non-sanitised, non-mechanical form of cleaning – functions as a correlative to the 'raking' of the countess's soul. Here, the discreet hum of the vacuum-cleaner does not so much shatter the spiritual resonance of its context as negate any relevance it might have, its bland modernity as destructive in its own way as the noise of the felled trees. Michel Chion has compared Bresson to Tati in that for both directors 'l'art de travailler les bruits et de les mettre en valeur est cohérent avec une certaine façon de *retenir les voix*'[16] (Chion 1982: 72) – a reversal of the customary primacy of speech over noise nowhere better exemplified than in this sequence.

Edwige has an assignation in a hotel of, precisely, Tati-like modernity with a left-wing bookseller to whom she afterwards speaks in scornful tones, not unlike those used by Marie to the grain merchant in *Balthazar*. Charles challenges Michel to guess whether it is Alberte or Edwige he loves more, declares in terms that recall Georges Bataille that his sole desire is for brutish ecstasy, and practises what he preaches with a female acquaintance who happens to be driving past, making a first unavailing attempt at suicide by drowning in her bathtub. He then decides to go and live with Edwige while her father is away. The bookseller, meanwhile, seems to be making a play for Alberte. This tangle of emotional shifts and hesitations is for me irritating and moving in almost equal measure. As Sémolué has implied, with the exception of Michel, stoically loyal to Alberte, the characters drift emotionally, unable even to articulate the reasons behind their feeling. In this respect *Le Diable* is the antithesis of Eustache's *La Maman et la putain*, which anatomises the affective disarray of the post-1968 generation through a carnivalesque proliferation of discourses none of which proves adequate to its task. Here, four years later, hypertrophy has yielded to entropy, logorrhea to near-aphasia. Bresson's 'contempt for *any* discourse' has nowhere been plainer.

The self-sustaining machinery of indecision is disrupted when

16 'the art of working upon sounds and bringing them to the fore is consistent with a certain way of *holding voices back*.'

Charles and Edwige spot Valentin, running away after stealing fruit from a shop. They feed and shelter him, but this is not to last long; the two young men go to spend the night in sleeping-bags listening to Monteverdi in a church, from which Valentin duly steals the collection box. (We may be briefly lured into believing that the music – *Ego dormio* – is, atypically for late Bresson, extra-diegetic, for it starts before we see the portable record-player the two have brought to the church with them.) He has absconded by the time the police arrive, so they take Charles in for questioning – an episode that triggers a deep depression, from which Edwige suggests only the renowned psychoanalyst Doctor Mime can rescue him. Mime's name is in ironic contrast to the centrality of language and the 'talking cure' in the Paris of the time – embodied above all by Jacques Lacan, whose notorious appetite for money is plainly alluded to when Charles peers at the wads of banknotes in the analyst's drawer. In almost every other respect, however, this scene is radically unlike any form of psychoanalysis one might encounter. Charles's friends telephone twice during the session, and are able to speak to Mime; Charles either stands or sits upright in a chair facing Mime, who appears not to have heard of the couch; he partially smokes a cigarette, for the first and only time in the film and judging by the way he does it the first and only time in his life; and the session consists of a string of only vaguely related questions and assertions, more appropriate to a social worker than to a psychoanalyst. Even Mime's less fatuous utterances, such as his view that the beatings Charles received in childhood have contributed to his suicidal state, are such blinding glimpses of the obvious as to evoke the pomposities of the police psychiatrist who 'explains' Norman Bates's behaviour in Hitchcock's *Psycho*. It is unclear how much direct experience of psychoanalysis Bresson had, but he cannot conceivably have been unaware of the ludicrousness of Mime's pre-new-age assertion that the years ahead will see major libidinal disruption for people in Charles's father's profession. Lacan famously stated that Catholics were impossible to psychoanalyse, and it is tempting to read this sequence as a Catholic's revenge on the analytic profession. Yet if it is a debunking of psychoanalysis it is a remarkably unsubtle one, the more so as the sequence leads directly into Charles's preparations for his suicide. Edwige's 'Il est sauvé'[17] – the last thing we hear any of Charles's friends other than Valentin say – thus appears unwittingly ironic, a credulous view of the analyst as shaman refuted even before it is articulated by Mime's effectively suggesting to Charles that he follow the example of the ancient Romans and ask a friend to do the deed for him.

An alternative possibility might be to read Edwige's remark as transcending the limitations of psychoanalysis and orthodox Catholic theology alike, gesturing towards a 'salvation' for Charles analogous to that suggested by the Monteverdi Magnificat at the end of *Mouchette*. Scarcely anything in the final sequence, however, encourages this reading; Charles's death is planned and worked towards with a chilly precision warmed only transiently when he hears Mozart piano music coming from a flat near Père-Lachaise cemetery. He buys a revolver from a hippy – peace and love indeed! – by the river, and visits Valentin in his squalid room to enlist and pay for his help. Valentin is unimpressed by Charles's reference to the ancient Romans ('Quelle antiquité romaine?'[18] is his only response), but willing to do what is asked of him. Charles drinks a brandy, the traditional last rite of the condemned, and walks past the flat from which Mozart can be heard. We almost certainly do not expect his resolve to be altered by this supreme archetype of western high culture as *raison d'être* of human existence (cf. the title of Godard's 1996 film about Bosnia, *Forever Mozart*). Such culture has figured throughout the film at best as narcotic (the appositely used *Ego dormio* in the last church scene), at worst as ammunition for Charles's *Weltschmerz* (the quotation on suicide from *The Brothers Karamazov* he copies into his diary). Here it offers a fleeting moment of calm but no more, and the two friends climb the cemetery wall in a grim reversal of the ending of *Un condamné*. Charles, standing near the grave of French Communist Party leader Maurice Thorez in what may be seen as a final gesture of political rejection, begins what he clearly intends to be a 'farewell speech' ('J'aurais cru que dans un

17 'He's saved.'
18 'What ancient Romans?'

moment aussi grave j'aurais des pensées sublimes. Tu veux que je te dise ...'),[19] but Valentin is unable even to hear out Charles's final act of nihilism, and shoots him – twice – in mid-sentence. He places the revolver in Charles's hand, helps himself to Charles's remaining money and runs off.

Le Diable is not only by a long way Bresson's most pessimistic film, it is one of the most pessimistic works of art known to me – in the same league as classical tragedy, Hardy's *Jude the Obscure* or Kieslowski's *A Short Film About Killing*. Perhaps it is the sheer unalleviated quality of its pessimism that can make it a difficult film to respond to emotionally; the ending of *Mouchette* has an ambiguity, that of *Lancelot* has been preceded by moments of love and hope, that make them more complex and, for me at any rate, more satisfying. Bresson's final film was also to end on an ambivalent note, as though *Le Diable* were as far as he was able to go down the route of nihilism.

L'Argent

Bresson's final film, shot in the summer of 1982 and released in 1983, brought to an end the longest gap in his work since that separating *Journal* from *Les Dames*, more than thirty years before. Like *Le Diable*, and even more ironically considering its title, *L'Argent* had difficulty in finding a producer (it was eventually co-produced by the television channel FR3 along with a French and a Swiss company), and was turned down by the *avance sur recettes* commission. Once more it was the personal intervention of the Culture Minister, this time the Socialist Jack Lang, that saved the project. Unkind suggestions were made that the casting of Lang's daughter Caroline in the principal female role of Élise may have had something to do with this – a view on which it would ill become me to comment here. The film shared, with Tarkovsky's *Nostalgia*, a Special Jury Prize at Cannes, news greeted with booing and cheering in almost equal volume (the boos may secretly have

19 "'I'd have expected to have sublime thoughts at such a grave moment. Shall I tell you ...'"

gladdened Orson Welles, who called Bresson on stage to receive his award and who had always been antipathetic to his work).

Élise is the wife of the film's central character, Yvon Targe, played by a young architect acquaintance of Bresson's, Christian Patey. Yvon is actually an amalgam of two characters in the Tolstoy novella *The Forged Coupon* on which the film is based – the wood-seller Ivan Mironov and the peasant Stepan Pelageyushkin, both like Bresson's protagonist poor working men caught up in the circulation of a forged currency note. (The 'coupon' of Tolstoy's title is the equivalent of a government bond.) Stepan murders Ivan for stealing his horse, and then kills first a family of innkeepers and then the gentle and truly Christian Maria Semyonovna before finding salvation through the Gospels in prison. The change in him is illustrated among other things by the willingness with which we are told 'he performed all the most difficult and unpleasant tasks, including the emptying and cleaning of the night-pail' (Tolstoy [c. 1856] 1985: 231) – a pre-echo of *Un condamné* which suggests that Bresson may well have read the novella many years before he filmed it.

The Forged Coupon is often regarded as the most 'Dostoevskyan' of Tolstoy's works, for its eschewal of conventional psychology and its transcendentally redemptive ending reminiscent of *Crime and Punishment* or *The Brothers Karamazov*. The epic historical sweep of the great Tolstoy novels is totally absent here; we are presented with a seemingly random collocation of individuals and groups bound together only by the circulation of material goods and currency. This is of course one of the master themes of the nineteenth-century French novel, Balzac and Zola (one of whose works is called *L'Argent*) in particular. There, however, it serves to indict as well as to justify the burgeoning of mercantile capitalism, without whose manifest evils there would after all be no story to tell. Tolstoy's novella deals less with the ills endemic in feudal society, shockingly present though these are, than with the paradox of individual salvation which makes it possible for one character to say of Stepan at the end: 'He murdered six people, but he's a holy man, I promise you' (Tolstoy [c. 1856] 1985: 253). Bresson's film, likewise, concerns itself as much with Yvon's descent and possible redemption as with the society in which these have taken place – perhaps because, as we have already seen in *Le Diable*, his work shows a profound pessimism about the institutions and discourses that seek to bring about social change.

This may seem to conflict with Sémolué's assertion that 'l'assassin, ce n'est pas Yvon: c'est l'argent'[20] (Sémolué 1993: 27). One resolution of this paradox, which shows it to be more apparent than real, is to be found in Prédal's view that the Bressonian *oeuvre* 'ne saurait jouer le rôle de miroir', or at least that if it does play such a role it is that of 'un miroir sans tain'[21] (Prédal 1983: 4). The notion of the mirror without tain – the silvered backing that makes it possible to view whatever 'is in' the mirror – has become widespread in Derridean discourse as a way of problematising the notion that texts in any straightforward way 'reflect' an already existing reality. Our analysis of key scenes from *Le Diable* has shown how Bresson's most recent work is indeed 'de plein-pied avec son époque'[22] (Prédal 1983: 5), while in no sense a realistic representation of it. Rather than reflection, it might make sense in this context to speak of refraction (literally, 'breaking up') – the murderous omnipresence of the cash nexus diffused and refracted through Yvon's increasingly desperate violence.

Alain Bergala, in a Lacanian formulation, speaks of money in *L'Argent* as 'la forme la plus pure ... de la circulation d'un désir qui n'aurait pas le temps de poisser dans une demande'[23] (Bergala 1983: 7), and the film's opening shot, of a bank cash-machine's chrome door sliding suavely shut, emphasises not only the rapidity and smoothness, but also the inexorability of that circulation in modern society. The filmic narratives of circulation that spring most readily to mind are perhaps those directed by Max Ophüls – *La Ronde* and *Madame de ...* . Desire in these films, however, is specifically sexual, which it is not in the world of *L'Argent* from which sexuality is almost entirely absent. *La Ronde's*

---

20 'the killer is not Yvon; it is money.'
21 '[it] cannot play the role of a mirror' ... 'a mirror without tain or silvering.'
22 'On an equal footing with its time.'
23 'the purest form ... of the circulation of a desire which has not had time to solidify into a demand.'

source play – Arthur Schnitzler's *Reigen* – indeed explicitly turns on the transmission of a venereal disease, euphemistically removed from the circular series of sexual encounters that make up the film. Sexual desire is more clearly imbricated with money in *Madame de …* , where it 'solidifies into [a] demand' in the shape of the precious earrings whose passing-on forms the film's narrative. Desire in the Ophüls films is, intermittently, a source of pleasure, delight, even rapture; in *L'Argent*, as in the pickpocket Michel's desire for money we never see him enjoying, it is, at best, a need fleetingly met or a craving temporarily alleviated. That desire which cannot give itself the time to solidify into demand belongs in the realm of Thanatos – that repetition whose repetition in Bresson's work finds its culminating instance here.

The relentless circulation of desire, in the form of money, finds a counterpart in the visual and spatial organisation of the film, similar to *Le Diable* in its fragmented, liminal quality. Clément Rosset observes that 'le lieu bressonien évoque souvent plutôt un "non-lieu" qu'un lieu véritable dans la mesure où il figure un passage d'un lieu à un autre, telles ces innombrables portes qui parcourent le film d'un bout à l'autre'[24] (Rosset 1997: 61). For Prédal, what is important for Bresson is 'les vecteurs de communication, les signes de la circulation, les rites de passage: portières qui claquent, cyclomoteurs qui démarrent, lettres qui arrivent sur la table des lectrices de la prison, couloirs, portes, fermetures de sécurité, menottes …'[25] (Prédal 1992: 124). 'Communication' here is not necessarily to be understood in a positive sense, for the two letters Yvon receives from Élise in prison communicate to him, first the death of their young daughter, then Élise's decision to break off all contact with him and build a new life – the opposite of Jeanne's letters to Michel.

24 'the Bressonian place is often more of a "non-place" than a real one, figuring as it does the passage from one place to another, as with the countless doors that we find all through the film.' (Translator's note: The French 'non-lieu' also means the dropping of criminal charges on the instruction of a judge).
25 'vectors of communication, signs of circulation, rites of passage: gates banging, mopeds starting up, letters arriving on the table for the prison censors to read, corridors, doors, security locks, handcuffs … .'

The prison scenes, like those in *Un condamné*, do not allow us any overall view of the building's topography; we are left with a sense of a structured but inscrutable environment, made up of a series of places and rites of passage – the yard where the prisoners arrive, the visiting room, the refectory and the infirmary. At the same time, these scenes, like those in the courtroom, have a powerfully realistic impact, not least because so little recent French cinema features court or jail scenes. There are a few reconstructions of courts set during the Occupation and Resistance years – Chabrol's *Une affaire de femmes*, Audiard's *Un héros très discret* – but for contemporary courtroom or prison drama of the kind so successful in Hollywood we have to go back to the 1950s and early 1960s (Cayatte's *Avant le déluge*, Becker's *Le Trou*, Clouzot's *La Vérité*). Such scenes clearly did not lend themselves to location filming and would probably have been tarred with the brush of the 'old-fashioned' cinema against which the New Wave did such spirited battle, which doubtless accounts for their scarcity. Bresson's courtroom and jail scenes have all the more impact in consequence, for the British or American viewer at any rate seeming close to a documentary reconstruction of institutions with which most of us presumably have little or no familiarity.

The film begins (after the credits) with the school student Norbert presenting himself in his father's study and pointing out that it is the first day of the month. The father duly hands him his monthly allowance – a dry and unemotional transaction that does not encourage us to view Norbert's family, whom we are not to see again after this sequence, as an exception to the dispiriting dysfunctionality of its late Bressonian counterparts. The amount is not enough, for Norbert has a debt to repay, but neither his father nor his mother is willing to help him. Thus it is that he visits classmate Martial (another in the Bresson repertoire of almost impossibly upmarket names), who shows him a forged 500-franc note. Where this has come from is not made plain, but that is because in a real sense it does not matter; the omnipresence of money, only a few minutes into the film, is already established as an inescapable given. The two friends set off on their mopeds for a photographic shop, where they succeed in passing off the note as genuine. The owner of the shop, whose wife – exactly as in the Tolstoy – has served the two young men, berates her for her gullibility. When she points out that he has recently accepted two such forgeries, he tranquilly replies that he will pass them on.

Hitherto, the film has been characterised by an atmosphere of calm opulence, apparent in the mellow green and beige the schoolboys wear and in Martial's aesthetic gesturing towards the plates in an art book ('C'est beau, un corps').[26] This is abruptly disturbed in the next shot, the first in all the director's work to depict an urban manual worker.[27] Rubber-gloved hands direct a pump full of diesel oil; only later do we discover that this is Yvon. The grimy soullessness of his toil is in stark contrast with what has gone before, a contrast accentuated by the fact that at first we do not see his face. The shop-owner pays Yvon with three 500-franc notes, but when he tries to use them one after another to pay for his meal in a restaurant all turn out to be forgeries. He is insulted and addressed as 'tu' – the intimate form, which in a situation such as this connotes contempt – by the waiter, whom he knocks to the ground. The shop-owner and his assistant Lucien deny all knowledge of Yvon when he seeks to prove his innocence, and Lucien is further to perjure himself when Yvon appears in court. He is found not guilty but strongly warned not to make allegations against 'respectable people'. The weighting of the judicial scales against poor working-class people is graphically and laconically illustrated – this, we should remember, in a France that the previous year had elected a Socialist president and government, and in a so-called post-industrial economy in which the urban working class was often seen as at best marginal, at worst obsolescent. Few French films of the time more effectively refute such a point of view.

The shop-owner slips an envelope into Lucien's pocket, containing money with which he can buy the suit he covets. We may be reminded here of Jacques's homily to Michel on how he might come to own a new suit or tie – the hypocrisy of bourgeois respectability substantially unchanged a quarter century down the line. Lucien's main anxiety is what judicial penalty he might incur for bearing false witness. Élise tries to encourage Yvon to ask for his old job back, but in an angry assertion of self-respect that is like an echo of the blow he struck in the restaurant he refuses to 'ramper vers eux comme un chien battu'.[28] A Camus-like revolt against the unjust and the absurd has never been more fiercely present in Bresson's work – not in *Mouchette* whose central character's suicide is escape as much as it is protest, nor even in *Le Diable* where Charles's despair is too all-encompassing and too consistently directed against himself.

At this point we leave Yvon and focus for a while on the two other strands of the plot. Lucien is dismissed, to the supposed sadness of both sides, for overcharging customers and pocketing the difference, a matter of little concern to him since he has equipped himself with copies of the keys to the shop and the safe. The shop-owner's wife, still smarting from having been outwitted, visits Martial and Norbert's school – clearly, and unsurprisingly, a private Catholic establishment, for it has a chaplain, which would be impossible in the strictly secular French-state system. The chaplain asks his religious education class their views on the ethics of passing forged notes; the first student claims to have none, the second does not know, and all Norbert is able to say is 'Me?' before leaving the room in confusion. This – the final appearance of institutionalised religion in Bresson's work – is as negative, as nihilistic even, as any of its predecessors. Matters between Norbert's mother and the shop-owner's wife are smoothed over with the aid of another envelope, which the latter verbally refuses but immediately pockets without demur. It is only for the working-class Yvon that money appears as a material necessity of life; elsewhere in this first part of the film, it functions as social lubricant and ethical alibi for an embarrassed bourgeoisie, facilitating contacts and exchanges that it thereby robs of any substantive reality they might have had.

28 'crawl back to them like a beaten dog.'

Behind Norbert's mother in the street we catch sight of Yvon (at first his legs only) – at once the return of a narrative strand we may almost have forgotten and an instance of the workings of chance and coincidence. He meets a friend on a café terrace who has an offer to make him – a malign inversion of Jacques's sanctimonious propositions to Michel, for the offer is to drive the getaway car for a bank robbery. The robbery sequence is among the subtlest yet most suspenseful in Bresson. Our attention is focused on what is happening through the reactions of a passer-by, distracted from the reading of his newspaper by the sight of armed police; we then see, in long-shot, a robber holding a woman hostage at gunpoint. Yvon drives off as shots are fired and there is a pile-up of cars. The sequence could not be further from conventional action filming, for what counts is the effect of the fragmented events we see and hear rather than any drama inherent in them. In this respect, and particularly bearing in mind the importance of the newspaper-reading man as focal point for spectator identification, it is reminiscent of some of the action sequences in Godard's *A bout de souffle*, in which the director himself plays the passer-by who turns Michel Poiccard in to the police near the end. Bresson is no more forthcoming about Godard's work than about that of any other film-maker (though he did opine, in my one meeting with him, that Godard 'certainly had something'), but it is tempting, if arguably mischievous, to detect a perhaps unconscious intertextual homage here.

Yvon is arrested, as we learn along with Élise, who is waiting at the police station. The words 'La cour!' – uttered to commence court proceedings in France – overlap with a shot of Élise seated, as though to suggest that machinery has been set in motion that goes beyond the control of those caught up in it. As Yvon, sentenced to three years' imprisonment, turns towards Élise, she walks away without meeting his gaze and picks up their daughter (Yvette) outside the courtroom. Yvon is not to see his daughter again – an example of how a Bressonian shot can acquire its full emotional weight and significance only retrospectively, in the context of the image's 'exchange value'. He sees Élise for what is to be the last time when she comes to visit him in prison, yet she is able to speak scarcely a word – a hesitancy explained when she tells him of Yvette's death in a letter, having been unable to do so face to face. The death of young children is famously cited by Dostoevsky's Ivan Karamazov as his prime reason for returning the ticket of eternal life to God. Bresson makes no such polemical use of it, yet it is a discreetly important motif in his work – most obviously in *Journal* and (stretching the term 'young' perhaps a little) in *Mouchette*, but also in *Balthazar* (Jacques's sister). Yvon's prostration is stoically received by his cellmates, more concerned with drinking bootleg alcohol from a flask they hide in a mattress.

Yvon's decline pursues a course of Job-like inexorability – a fight with other prisoners leading to solitary confinement, Élise's final breaking-off, his saving of sedative pills until he has enough for an overdose, his recovery in the infirmary as a nurse asks with cruel kindness 'Ça va, Yvon?' The elliptical terseness of Bresson's filming, and its stress on material detail (such as the piece of metal Yvon obsessively scrapes across the floor of his cell), makes these grim scenes the reverse of melodramatic. Yvon is joined in prison by Lucien, seen getting out of a police van in a shot that rhymes with the one in which we saw Yvon's arrival. The first attempt at some kind of discursive response to all we have seen is no more convincing than its precursors in *Le Diable*; Yvon's new cellmate theatrically denounces the 'dieu visible' of money and avers that 'le bonheur universel sera terriblement chiant',[29] a statement curiously at odds with the political affiliation we might be tempted to deduce from the Communist Party-published book we see him holding. The noise of a vacuum-cleaner in this scene further stresses its kinship with *Le Diable*, but the discursive futility that film develops at length is here much more succinctly suggested – a reflection among other things of the decline in radical political speech and activity in the years separating the two.

Lucien tries to persuade Yvon to join his escape attempt, but Yvon would rather kill him than do any such thing. If the relationship between the imprisoned Yvon and Élise is the anti-*Pickpocket*, that between Lucien and Yvon here is the antithesis of

29 'universal happiness will be a terrible pain in the arse.'

that which develops between Fontaine and Jost. It is as if Bresson were re-enacting and destroying those aspects of his earlier films that might seem to provide a glimmer of hope for Yvon, an impression strengthened when his cellmate, hearing that Lucien has smashed up his cell, tells Yvon in words that might come straight from *Un condamné*: 'Quelqu'un, de loin, te protège', only for Yvon to respond: 'Je n'ai ni parent, ni ami, ni femme'.[30]

On his release Yvon goes to a hotel whose door we see in close-up. A further close-up, of a washbasin filled with bloody water, is followed by a shot of Yvon emptying the till. This scene carries the elliptical use of narrative space further than almost anything else in the director's work – the murder of the couple seen only through its aftermath, the claustrophobia we might expect to have been dispelled by Yvon's release from prison on the contrary nightmarishly intensified. Part of that nightmare resides in the dearth of topographical detail, making it impossible for us to construct a coherent view of the hotel and leading us to feel that Yvon has been released from a space where he knew only too well where he was into one where he does not know where he is at all.

This makes the next part of the film, set in the countryside, a healing contrast to all that has gone before. Yvon sees a grey-haired woman withdrawing money from the village post-office, and follows her across a bridge over a stream whose running water is the gentlest sound in the film. He makes his way into her house, where we see her taking care of an elderly man and a sickly adolescent. When he tells her of his killings, she responds that if she were God she would pardon everybody – the meekness of the Bressonian *femme douce* implicitly assimilated to that of Christ. We are to learn that she is a widow, the elderly man (a piano teacher turned alcoholic) is her father and the boy her nephew, of whom she seems to take more care than his own briefly espied parents. Her father slaps her angrily as she brings coffee to Yvon; the idyllic surroundings begin to seem a cruel counterpoint to her life of drudgery and ill treatment. Yet, between this and Yvon's

---

30 'Somebody, from a distance, is protecting you.' ... 'I have no relations, no friends, no wife.'

furtively menacing explorations of the house, there is a moment that seems to me to contain a possibility of something else, something better, which the film's ending in its almost unfathomable ambiguity does not altogether deny. This is when Yvon helps the woman to hang out washing and shells hazelnuts which she eats – a scene with unmistakable echoes of *laborare est orare* and of George Herbert, and one whose pastoral simplicity is almost Beethovenian. (I think here not only of the Sixth Symphony but of the slow movement of the Opus 132 String Quartet – *Heiliger Dankgesang eines Genesenen*, the holy song of thanksgiving of one restored).

Yet the next sequence returns us to the nightmare night-time world of the inn. The woman's father and the boy's parents are seen, murdered with an axe, lying across the staircase. The widow sits calmly in her bed, as if awaiting release; Yvon, raising the axe one last deadly time, cries: 'Où est l'argent?'[31] – a question to which Bresson has said his film implies the answer: 'Everywhere'. We then see the axe thrown into a stream whose waters it reddens, and Yvon standing motionless beside a wall.

The final sequence is a direct evocation of *Crime and Punishment*, in which Raskolnikov's confession acts as perhaps the supreme Pascalian bet on the possibility of redeeming the irredeemable. Yvon presents himself to policemen in a café and admits to the killings of the hotel-keepers and of an entire family. An inquisitive group masses around the café door, from which Yvon emerges flanked by police. Yet the bystanders' heads do not follow him, as we might logically expect; they continue to gaze through the open door, into (though not 'at') the café. It is almost impossible to avoid reading this final shot in the entire Bressonian *œuvre* (which is not followed by the word 'Fin' on the screen) as some kind of metonymic summary or distillation, and equally impossible, as so often with this film-maker, to attribute a single sense or value to it. The best that can be done is perhaps to set down, in a hesitant and fragmentary way, certain reflections the shot stimulates in me:

31 'Where is [the] money?'

- It says something about the constitutive incompleteness of Bresson's work, which leaves, in this case doubtless for ever, its audience looking for (a) 'more' that is perhaps less within the work than within themselves.

- It suggests that there is no clear and unequivocal way of imputing degrees of ethical responsibility for human beings' actions. The crowd gather, presumably, to see the murderer; when they see 'only' Yvon instead, this is somehow not enough, so they look beyond him for/towards the absolute evil he has clearly failed to represent. In this respect at least *L'Argent* is a not entirely pessimistic film, for Yvon as incarnation of evil is a far less convincing figure than Gérard or even Mordred.

- If the bystanders figure the audience, their turned and motionless heads suggest not only that they may be wanting something more out of the film, but that they are possibly seeking a way back into it. *L'Argent* poses, as very few films do, questions of good, evil and justice – and the greater and still more troubling question of whether such questions have anything that might be called a sense. The turned heads will clearly find no answer, in an unproblematic sense, to questions such as these; but they may be looking for a place from which an answer might be articulated. Now that it is clear that *L'Argent* was Bresson's last film, such a reading of the final shot becomes more inviting than ever, making it less a closure than a perpetual opening, or even a Möbius-like looping back into a body of work whose component parts can best be understood in their often complex and contradictory relation with one another.

References

Augustine, Saint ([397] 1992), *Confessions*, Oxford and New York, Oxford University Press (World's Classics).

Bergala, Alain (1983), 'Bresson, *L'Argent* et son spectateur', *Cahiers du cinéma*, nos. 348–9.

Chion, Michel (1982), *La Voix au cinéma*, Paris, Cahiers du cinéma.

Daney, Serge (1996), *La Rampe*, Paris, Cahiers du cinéma.

Fassbinder, Rainer Werner (1998), in James Quandt (ed.), *Robert Bresson*, Toronto, Cinematheque Ontario.

Freud, Sigmund ([1930] 1961), *Civilisation and its Discontents*, New York and London, Norton.

Oudart, Jean-Pierre (1977), 'Modernité de Robert Bresson', *Cahiers du cinéma*, nos. 279–80.

Prédal, René (1983), *Cinéma 83*, no. 294.

Prédal, René (1992), *Robert Bresson: l'aventure intérieure, L'Avant-scène cinéma*, nos. 408–9.

Rosset, Clément (1997), in *Robert Bresson: Hommage*, Milan and Paris, Mazzotta/ Cinémathèque française.

Sémolué, Jean (1993), *Bresson ou l'acte pur des métamorphoses*, Paris, Flammarion.

Tolstoy, Leo ([c. 1856] 1985), *The Kreutzer Sonata and Other Stories*, Harmondsworth, Penguin.

Truffaut, François and Latil-Le Dantec, Mireille (1997), 'Entretien sur Robert Bresson', in *Robert Bresson: Hommage*, Milan and Paris, Mazzotta/Cinémathèque française.

Filmography

(It should be noted that running times tend to be given differently from one source-text to the next, and that films shown on television are often slightly shortened.)

Affaires publiques[1] 1934 (*Public Affairs*)

25 min.
Producer: Arc-Film
Script: Bresson (the playwright André Josset helped with the dialogues)
Photography: Nicolas Toporkoff
Sets: Pierre Charbonnier
Music: Jean Wiener
Sound: Robert Petiot
Cast: Beby (the chancellor of Crocandie), Andrée Servilanges (the princess of Mirandie), Marcel Dalio (announcer/sculptor/head of the fire brigade/admiral), Gilles Margaritis

Les Anges du péché 1943 (*Angels of Sin*)

97 min.
Producer: Synops-Roland Tual
Script: Bresson, based on an idea by R. L. Bruckberger and with dialogues by Jean Giraudoux
Assistant director: Frédéric Liotier
Photography: Philippe Agostini

---

1 This is generally referred to as *Les Affaires publiques*, but the Cinémathèque print I viewed has no definite article.

Sets: René Renoux
Music: Jean-Jacques Grünewald
Sound: René Louge
Cast: Renée Faure (Anne-Marie), Jany Holt (Thérèse), Sylvie (the prioress), Marie-Hélène Dasté (Mother Saint-Jean), Mila Parély (Madeleine), Yolande Laffon (Madame Lamaury, Anne-Marie's mother), Paula Dehelly (Mother Dominique), Louis Seigner (prison governor), Georges Colin (chief of police)

Les Dames du Bois de Boulogne 1945 (*Ladies of the Bois de Boulogne*)

90 min.
Producer: Films Raoul Ploquin
Script: Bresson, based on Diderot's *Jacques le fataliste*, with dialogues by Jean Cocteau
Assistant directors: Roger Spiri-Mercanton, Raymond Bailly, Paul Barbellion
Photography: Philippe Agostini
Sets: Max Douy
Music: Jean-Jacques Grünewald
Sound: René Louge, Robert Ivonnet, Lucien Legrand
Cast: Paul Bernard (Jean), Maria Casarès (Hélène), Élina Labourdette (Agnès), Lucienne Bogaert (Agnès's mother), Jean Marchat (Jacques), Yvette Étiévant (Hélène's servant)

Journal d'un curé de campagne 1951 (*Diary of a Country Priest*)

110 min.
Producer: UGC
Script: Bresson, based on Bernanos's *Journal d'un curé de campagne*
Assistant director: Guy Lefranc
Photography: Léonce-Henri Burel
Sets: Pierre Charbonnier
Music: Jean-Jacques Grünewald
Sound: Jean Rieul
Cast: Claude Laydu (the *curé* of Ambricourt), Armand Guibert (the *curé* of Torcy), Marie-Monique Arkell – real name Rachel Berendt, a stage actress who had appeared in Giraudoux – (the countess), Nicole Ladmiral (Chantal), Jean Riveyre (the count), Jean Danet (Olivier), Nicole Maurey (mademoiselle Louise), Gaston Séverin (the canon), Antoine Balpêtré (Doctor Delbende), Martine Lemaire (Séraphita

Dmouchel), Bernard Hubrenne (Dufréty), Yvette Étiévant (Dufréty's companion)

Un condamné à mort s'est échappé 1956 (aka *Le Vent souffle où il veut*) (*A Man Escaped*) (*The Wind Bloweth where it Listeth*)

95 min.
Producer: Jean Thuillier, Jean Poiré (Gaumont, Nouvelles éditions de films)
Script: Bresson, based on a text by André Devigny
Photography: Léonce-Henri Burel
Assistant directors: Jacques Ballanche, Michel Clément
Sets: Pierre Charbonnier
Music: Kyrie from Mozart's C Minor Mass (conductor: J. Dishenhaus)
Sound: Pierre-André Bertrand
Cast: François Leterrier (Fontaine), Charles le Clainche (Jost), Maurice Beerblock (Blanchet), Roland Monod (the pastor), Jacques Ertaud (Orsini), Rober Tréherne (Terry), Jean-Paul Delhumeau (Henbard)

Pickpocket 1959

75 min.
Producer: Agnès Delahaie
Script: Bresson
Assistant directors: Jacques Ballanche, Michel Clément
Photography: Léonce-Henri Burel
Sets: Pierre Charbonnier
Music: Lulli
Sound: Antoine Archimbaud
Cast: Martin Lassalle (Michel), Marika Green (Jeanne), Pierre Lemayrie (Jacques), Jean Pelegri (police inspector), Dolly Scal (Michel's mother), Hassagi and Pierre Étaix (other pickpockets)

Le Procès de Jeanne d'Arc 1962 (*Trial of Joan of Arc*)

65 min.
Producer: Agnès Delahaie
Script: Bresson (based on transcripts of the trial)
Assistant directors: Marcel Ugols, Alain Ferrari, Serge Roullet, Hugo Santiago
Photography: Léonce-Henri Burel
Sets: Pierre Charbonnier

Sound: Antoine Archimbaud
Cast: Florence Carrez (Jeanne), Jean-Claude Fourneau (Cauchon), Roger Honorat (Jean Beaupère), Richard Pratt (Warwick), Marc Jacquier (Lemaître), Michel Hérubel Isambart)

Au hasard Balthazar 1966 (*Balthazar*)

95 min.
Producer: Parc Film, Argos Films (Anatole Dauman), Athos Films, Svensk Filmindustri, Swedish Film Institute, Mag Bodard
Script: Bresson
Assistant directors: Sven Frostenson, Jacques Kébadian, Claude Miller
Photography: Ghislain Cloquet
Sets: Pierre Charbonnier
Music: Schubert, Piano Sonata no. 20 (Jean-Noël Barbier)
Sound: Antoine Archimbaud, Jacques Carrère
Cast: Anne Wiazemsky (Marie), François Lafarge (Gérard), Walter Green (Jacques), Jean-Claude Guilbert (Arnold), Pierre Klossowski (the grain merchant), Philippe Asselin (Marie's father), Nathalie Joyaut (Marie's mother), Marie-Claire Frémont (the baker's wife), François Sullerot (the baker), Jean-Joël Barbier (the Dean), Mylène Weyergans (the nurse), Guy Bréjac (the vet), Tord Paag, Roger Fjellstrom, Sven Frostenson (Gérard's associates)

Mouchette 1967

82 min.
Producer: Argos Films, Parc Film (Anatole Dauman)
Script: Bresson, based on Bernanos's *Nouvelle histoire de Mouchette*
Assistant directors: Mylène Van der Mersch, Jacques Kébadian
Photography: Ghislain Cloquet
Sets: Pierre Guffroy
Music: Monteverdi, Magnificat from the Venetian Vespers, conducted by the Reverend Émile Martin
Sound: Séverin Frankiel, Jacques Carrère
Cast: Nadine Nortier (Mouchette), Jean-Claude Guilbert (Arsène), Paul Hébert (Mouchette's father), Marie Cardinal (Mouchette's mother), Jean Vimenet (Mathieu), Marie Susini (Mathieu's wife), Martine Trichet (Louisa), Liliane Princet (the schoolteacher), Raymonde Chabrun (the grocer), Suzanne Huguenin (old woman who loves the dead)

Une femme douce 1969 (*A Gentle Creature*)

88 min.

Producer: Parc Film, Marianne Production (Mag Bodard)
Script: Bresson, based on Dostoevsky's *A Gentle Creature*
Assistant directors: Mylène Van der Mersch, Jacques Kébadian
Photography: Ghislain Cloquet
Sets: Pierre Charbonnier
Music: Purcell, Jacques Wiener
Sound: Jacques Maumont, Jacques Lebreton, Urbain Loiseau
Cast: Dominique Sanda (the woman), Guy Frangin (the man), Jane
Lobre (Anna), Claude Ollier (the doctor)

Quatre nuits d'un rêveur 1972 (*Four Nights of a Dreamer*)

90 min.

Producer: Victoria Film, Albina Film, Film dell'Orso
Script: Bresson, based on Dostoevsky's *White Nights*
Assistant directors: Mylène Van der Mersch, André Bitoun, Jean-
Pierre Ghys, Munni Kabir
Photography: Pierre Lhomme, Ghislain Cloquet for the 'film-within-
a-film'
Sets: Pierre Charbonnier
Sound: Roger Letellier
Cast: Isabelle Weingarten (Marthe), Guillaume des Forêts (Jacques),
Jean-Maurice Monnoyer (the tenant), Aline Dumontet (Marthe's
mother), Jérôme Massart (Jacques's art-school friend), Patrick
Jouanné (the gangster)

Lancelot du lac 1974 (*Lancelot of the Lake*)

85 min.

Producer: Jean-Pierre Rassam, Jean Yanne, François Rochat (Mara-
Films, Laser-Productions, ORTF, Gerico Sound)
Script: Bresson
Assistant directors: Mylène Van der Mersch, Robert Baroody, Bernard
Cohn
Photography: Pasqualino de Santis
Sets: Pierre Charbonnier
Sound: Bernard Bats, Jacques Carrère
Cast: Luc Simon (Lancelot), Laura Duke Condominas (Guenièvre),
Humbert Balsan (Gauvain), Vladimir Antolek-Orosek (Arthus),
Patrick Bernard (Mordred), Arthur de Monalembert (Lionel)

Le Diable probablement 1977 *(The Devil, Probably)*

96 min.
Producer: Sunchild (Stéphane Tchalgadjieff), G. M. F.
Script: Bresson
Assistant directors: Mylène Van der Mersch, Thierry Bodin, Humbert Balsan, Eric Deroo, Machaud de Cordon
Photography: Pasqualino de Santis
Sets: Éric Simon
Sound: Georges Prat
Cast: Antoine Monnier (Charles), Henri de Maublanc (Michel), Tina Irissari (Alberte), Laetitia Carcano (Edwige), Nicolas Deguy (Valentin), Geoffroy Gaussen (the bookseller), Régis Hanrion (Mime, the psychoanalyst), Nathalie Delannoy (the woman who gives Charles the chocolates)

L'Argent 1983 *(Money)*

85 min.
Producer: Marion's Films (Jean-Marie Henchoz), FR3, Eos Film (Switzerland)
Script: Bresson, based on Tolstoy's *The Forged Coupon*
Assistant directors: Mylène Van der Mersch, Thierry Bodin, Pascal Bony
Photography: Pasqualino de Santis, Emmanuel Machel
Sets: Pierre Guffroy
Sound: Jean-Louis Ughetto, Luc Yersin
Cast: Christian Patey (Yvon Targe), Caroline Lang (Élise Targe), Sylvie Van den Elsen (grey-haired woman), Didier Baussy (owner of camera shop), Béatrice Tabourin (his wife), Michel Briguet (grey-haired woman's father), Vincent Risterucci (Lucien), Marc-Ernest Fourneau (Norbert), André Cler (Norbert's father), Claude Cler (Norbert's mother), Bruno Lapeyre (Martial), Jeanne Aptekman (Yvette), François-Marie Banier (Yvon's cellmate)

Select Bibliography

Arnaud, Philippe (1986), *Robert Bresson*, Paris, Cahiers du cinéma. Penetrating analysis from a largely Lacanian perspective. Invaluable in clarifying Oudart's sometimes tortuous reading of *Le Procès de Jeanne d'Arc*.

Cameron, Ian (ed.) (1969), *The Films of Robert Bresson*, London, Studio Vista. Long since out of print and overtaken by later theoretical developments, but the first English-language collection of work on Bresson.

Droguet, Robert (1966), *Robert Bresson*, Premier Plan 42, Lyon. Long out of print. Contains some succulent *Positif*-style invective.

Estève, Michel (1983), *Robert Bresson: la passion du cinématographe*, Paris, Albatros. Sound, thematic overview from a leading Bernanos scholar.

Godard, Jean-Luc (1966), 'Le Testament de Balthazar,' *Cahiers du cinéma*, 177: 58–9. Idiosyncratic, even perverse, but deeply illuminating on the possible hidden philosophical agenda of Bresson's work.

Guth, Paul (1989), *Autour des 'Dames du bois de Boulogne'*, Paris, Ramsay. Reissue of an autobiographical account fascinating more for its evocation of the constraints of wartime film-making than for any specifically cinematic light it may shed on Bresson.

Hanlon, Lindley (1986), *Fragments: Bresson's Film Style*, Cranbury, London and Toronto, Associated University Presses. Sometimes lengthy and laboured, but does a decent job of situating Bresson's middle and late work within a post-modernist narratological perspective.

Jones, Kent (1999). *L'Argent*, London, British Film Institute. A valuable and concise monograph.

Oudart, Jean-Pierre (1969), 'La Suture,' *Cahiers du cinéma*, no. 211. Bresson is the starting-point for what was to become a key text of neo-Lacanian cinematic theory.

Positif (1996), no. 430. The *Dossier Robert Bresson* in this number represents something like a settling of accounts with one who for a long time was the target of much anti-clerical hostility from the journal. There is a particularly good piece from Nicole Brenez comparing Bresson with Eustache, Garrel and Hellman.

Prédal, René (1992), *Robert Bresson: l'aventure intérieure*, *L'Avant-scène cinéma*, nos. 408–9. A workmanlike overview of the *œuvre*.

Quandt, James (ed.) (1998), *Robert Bresson*, Toronto, Cinematheque Ontario. A beautifully presented collection of more than 600 pages, including three interviews with the director, the views of thirty or so film-makers on him and important critical material hitherto unavailable in English.

Robert Bresson: Éloge, (1997) Milan/Paris, Mazzotta/Cinémathèque française. A collection – less hagiographic than its title might suggest – of perspectives on the director's work from figures as disparate as Julien Gracq, Sacha Guitry and François Truffaut.

Schrader, Paul (1972), *Transcendental Style in Film: Ozu, Bresson, Dreyer*, Los Angeles/London, University of California Press. From Scorsese's alter-ego, a view of Bresson that transcends theological barriers to consider his work side by side with the greatest directors in the Buddhist and Protestant traditions.

Sémolué, Jean (1993), *Bresson ou l'acte pur des métamorphoses*, Paris, Flammarion. Probably the best overall study of the director's work for a non-specialist readership. Erudite yet accessible.

Sloan, Jane (1983); *Robert Bresson: A Guide to References and Resources*, Boston, G. K. Hall. An invaluable and comprehensive survey of material on Bresson from the beginnings up to 1980.

Index